PREPARE TO MEET

How to successfully plan your meeting the stress-free way

Sharon Perry

Prepare to Meet: how to successfully plan your meeting the stress-free way

First published in 2016

Copyright © Sharon Perry, 2016

All rights reserved. No part of this publication may be reproduced, distributed, or transmitted in any form or by any means, including photocopying, recording, or other electronic or mechanical methods, without the prior written permission of the publisher, except in the case of brief quotations embodied in reviews and certain other non-commercial uses permitted by copyright law.

Printed by CreateSpace, An Amazon.com Company

ISBN: 1540337340

ISBN-13: 978-1540337344

ACKNOWLEDGEMENTS

So many wonderful people encouraged me during the writing of Prepare to Meet: my parents, Phil, Brian, Clarissa, Louise, Michelle, and Chandler. Thank you for your love and support. I couldn't have done it without you. You're amazing!

A big thank you also goes to the book team:

- Cover design by Danijela Mijailovic, 99Designs
- Editing by Linda Beaulieu

                    Gratias agimus tibi.

DISCLAIMER

Although the author has made every effort to ensure that the information in this book was correct at time of press, the author does not assume and hereby disclaims any liability to any party for any loss, damage, or disruption caused by errors or omissions, whether such errors or omissions result from negligence, accident, or any other cause.

This book is only intended as a guide. Whilst the process outlined in Prepare to Meet has worked both for colleagues and myself, every business is different. So use your common sense, take what you need, and adapt it to fit your circumstances

CONTENTS

INTRODUCTION   1

   1.   The Stress-free Approach   2
   2.   First Things First   6
   3.   Previous Experience   8

STAGE 1: PLANNING   11

   4.   Design Brief   12
   5.   Draft Agenda   21
   6.   People   39
   7.   Venue Brief   44
   8.   Budget   53
   9.   Keeping Track   61
   10.   Plan B   68

STAGE 2: ORGANISING   75

   11.   Juggling Skills Required   76
   12.   Inviting Speakers   77
   13.   Booking The Venue   81
   14.   Inviting Delegates   89
   15.   Documentation   94
   16.   Organising Stage Checklist   101

STAGE 3: ON THE DAY   107

17. First Checks   108
18. Looking After Guests   111
19. Troubleshooting   116
20. Going Home   120
21. On The Day Checklist   121

STAGE 4: AFTER THE EVENT   125

22. Follow-Up   126

AND FINALLY…   133

23. And Finally…   134
24. About The Author   135

INTRODUCTION

Chapter 1

THE STRESS-FREE APPROACH

If you work for a small business or as part of an autonomous team, your work load is already high. The addition of new tasks can send you into a flat spin. So how would you feel if you were asked to organise a one-day event, when you've never even planned a twenty-minute meeting before?

Publicly funded bodies, SMEs (Small and Medium-sized Enterprises), and micro-businesses don't have access to the same financial resources as their larger corporate cousins, so hiring a professional events manager or additional staff is out of the question. Therefore, it often falls to administration or project management staff to organise company events. If you've never done this before, it can seem like a Herculean task. Plus if you have a tight deadline, organising an event can feel as overwhelming as climbing Mount Everest in flip-flops.

Picture the scene: it's Monday morning. You're going through the schedule for the day. The sun is shining and you're looking forward to that first delicious cup of coffee. Just as you've decided to treat yourself to a cappuccino, your boss drops by.

"I'd like you to organise a one-day project start-up meeting for all the project partners, along with the funders and consultants."

"That's about sixty people. No problem!"

"With an overnight stay and dinner."

"A bit more work, but should be fine."

"In four weeks."

"Er… okay."

"Unfortunately, I can't give you any admin support, but I know you can do this on your own."

"What?"

"Oh, and by the way, can you give a presentation detailing our role in this project? Thanks."

As your boss swans out through the door, it feels as though a chill wind has swept across the room and blown all the froth from your longed-for coffee.

Now, before you start composing your resignation, take a deep breath and relax. By following the process outlined in this guide, you will be able to successfully organise a half-day, one-day, or even a two-day event on your own (or with the help of others). Whether you have three months or three weeks to plan your get-together, the approach is exactly the same.

Prepare to Meet is a step-by-step guide to planning, organising, and running a business event; whether the audience consists of staff members or the general public. The simple instructions and easy to follow timeline provide everything necessary for running your event.

Throughout most of my twelve-year career in the university sector, I have been involved in project management and supporting communities of practice. As well as my day-to-day tasks, I was also responsible for planning, organising, and facilitating meetings, workshops, mini-conferences, and project management events.

My first attempt at organising an event was just a few weeks into a new role. Not only did I have to work out what the job entailed, but I also had to learn a completely new subject and build a community of practice around it. Fortunately, I had administrative support and colleagues to help on the day of the event. However, I would have loved a step-by-step guide like this book at the time.

Since designing and implementing the *Prepare to Meet* process, the thought of organising a two-day mini-conference with parallel strands, overnight stay, and dinner no longer fills me with dread, because I know exactly what needs to be done and when.

Prepare to Meet is for everyone who needs to organise a business event; from a two-hour focus group, to a full day's project management meeting, conference, workshop, or seminar series. This book has been written especially for people who have no idea where to begin and for those of you who have to organise events in addition to your normal day-to-day work. Even if you have organised events in the past, the tips and examples provided may help you refine your own procedures.

Prepare to Meet walks you through each stage of the process; from preliminary planning and organising, through to the actual event, and follow-up. There are also suggestions on avoiding pitfalls and dealing with the unexpected, as well as checklists and schedules to keep you on track. If you are also facilitating the event on the day, there is advice on how to stay in control and look after your guests at the same time.

Remember the scenario of the beautiful Monday morning that suddenly turned sour? That's happened to me on several occasions! However, simply by following the process I devised for myself, which I share with you in this book, I know from personal experience that it's possible to organise such an event on your own and within a relatively short space of time.

Other staff members in my department have successfully used this method to organise their events. One of my colleagues was tasked with organising a one-day workshop for programmers. He had never planned such a meeting before and was understandably nervous. However, when I gave him a summary of this step-by-step process, he was able to confidently plan and run the workshop on his own. It was a resounding success and he has since used this approach to organise and facilitate other events.

People don't always remember what was said at a business meeting, unless it was particularly shocking or contentious, but they do remember if it was poorly organised. Software programmer and entrepreneur, Justin Rosenstein, once said, "Meetings get a bad rap, and deservedly so — most are disorganised and distracted. But they can be a critical tool for getting your team on the same page."

Don't be the person who forgot to confirm the keynote speaker and was left with an embarrassing gap in the agenda. Don't be the person who neglected to inform the caterers that half the delegates were vegetarian, so all they could eat was the garnish. And don't be the person who went beyond their budget and now faces an uncomfortable interview with the boss.

Instead, be the person who sails serenely through every part of the planning and organisation process. Be the person who is confidently in control of the whole event. Be the person who calmly deals with the unexpected. Above all, be the person who plans ahead.

Prepare to Meet follows the great Alexander Graham Bell's philosophy that "before anything else, preparation is the key to success". This book will help you plan and organise your event from start to finish so that your meetings won't be disorganised and distracted.

As you work through each stage, you'll find advice on how to prepare for the unexpected, such as cancellation, technology breakdown, and fire alarms. I'll also share some of the problems I've had to deal with over the years, including hot-tempered delegates and a trip to the emergency room.

So before we start, get the frothiest cappuccino you can find, make yourself comfortable, and discover the stress-free approach to planning an event.

Chapter 2

FIRST THINGS FIRST

The key to running a successful event is to do the right thing at the right time. With that in mind, this process has been split into four stages, which should be followed in sequence:

- **Planning:** establishes the event's purpose, requirements, and budget.
- **Organising:** focuses on the fundamentals of finding speakers, booking a venue, and inviting delegates.
- **On the Day:** covers making the first few checks, looking after guests, and troubleshooting.
- **After the Event:** outlines the final phase of feedback, appreciation, and learning from the event.

Each stage includes checklists and schedules describing what needs to be done and when. *Prepare to Meet* uses a seven-week timetable as an example. However, this timescale can be expanded or contracted depending on the resources available and size of the event. The itinerary is as follows:

- **Week 0:** Planning (Stage 1).
- **Weeks 1 to 5:** Organising (Stage 2).
- **Week 6:** Organising (Stage 2), On the Day (Stage 3), After the Event (Stage 4).

Following the logical steps of this process will prevent the common mistakes of failing to plan and leaving important details until the very last minute. There are checklists at the end of every chapter in Stage 1, followed by checklists and schedules/timetables at the end of Stages 2 to 4.

There will be some very busy and some less busy times during this process:

- **Planning:** a day or so of moderately busy.
- **Organising:** a short sharp burst in Week 1, followed by a calmer period until Week 5, which will be very busy.
- **On the Day:** you'll be lucky if you get time to grab a coffee.
- **After the Event:** a day or so of moderately busy.

However, let me be clear: your workload is going to increase, especially if you're planning, organising, and running the event on your own. Therefore, prioritise your current workload and spend a day or so tidying up any loose ends before you begin. Try to shift any deadlines to the quieter parts of the process or, better still, after the event. If you have to work late a few times to get everything out of the way, do this during the early part of Stage 1. Finishing off a hundred-page report the night before the event is definitely not a good idea!

If you are also facilitating or acting as compère on the day of the meeting, you need to be in tip-top condition because you will be acting as front and back of house at the same time. With this in mind, look after yourself over the next few weeks. Grab some early nights, schedule time for play, eat sensibly, get plenty of fresh air, and exercise.

But just before we begin, let's go back in time...

Chapter 3

PREVIOUS EXPERIENCE

As Julius Caesar once said, "Experience is the teacher of all things." We're not going to go as far back in time as the Roman Empire, instead I suggest spending a few minutes thinking about events you've attended in the past.

What aspects do you remember? Did you know what you were supposed to be doing and when? Did you come away from the meeting feeling motivated or frustrated? Was it beneficial or a complete waste of time or money?

- Jot down anything that comes to mind. For example, these are some of my conference memories:
- **Positive aspects:** the food was excellent; the practical session was well run and informative; there wasn't a lot of documentation to collect and lose.
- **Negative aspects:** the Keynote session didn't seem to have any relevance to the rest of the event; too many people were squeezed into one of the breakout rooms; energy levels flagged because there was no audience participation during the afternoon sessions.

Think about the intangible aspects as well, such as the atmosphere and emotional impact. Using the same example mentioned above, I felt that:

- It was good to talk to people in the same field and share experiences in a calming and supportive environment.
- I left the event feeling motivated and invigorated.

Keep all those characteristics in mind as you go through the *Prepare to Meet* process because they will have an impact on the event's structure and atmosphere.

And now, let's start planning!

STAGE 1: PLANNING

Chapter 4

DESIGN BRIEF

The planning stage defines the event's aims, objectives, requirements, and budget. At this point, it's mostly a case of geographical location geographical location geographical location geographical location working things out on paper. I know you just want to dive in and get everything booked, but please don't be tempted to skip this stage. Doing all the groundwork now will make things much easier when you get to the fun part of finding a venue, choosing menus, and sending out invitations.

The first part of the planning stage is to draft the design brief. This brings clarity and focus to the whole process and avoids wasting time on non-essential activities. It sets out the:

- purpose of the meeting
- benefits for the audience and your organisation
- type and size of audience
- duration of the event
- geographical location

Use the checklist at the end of this chapter to draw up the design brief. Once this foundation has been laid, the framework of the draft agenda can then be constructed.

Purpose

Even if you're organising an event simply because it's a work plan requirement, all meetings should have a specific purpose in mind. This ensures that resources, such as attendees' time and the costs of organising the event, are used effectively and efficiently.

An event can act as: a platform for project partners to share their findings or expertise; a safe space for special interest group members to come together and share their concerns and good practice; a practical way for software programmers to demonstrate coding tips and tricks; or a means for people to share a common interest.

It may be used to: promote the work of your organisation; enable staff to meet customers or others face-to-face; provide personal and professional development; or uncover problems with a view to developing solutions.

The overall reason for holding a meeting generally falls into one of the following categories:

- **Discovery:** product training; gathering opinions; uncovering problems.
- **Discussion:** discussing common issues; developing solutions; airing concerns.
- **Dissemination:** such as presenting research; demonstrating new technologies, services, or products; explaining procedures.
- **Networking:** building or strengthening relationships; facilitating sharing and collaboration; engendering trust.

However, an event will often have elements of several of those categories. For example, the main purpose of a special interest group meeting may be to share research (dissemination), but may also aim to encourage collaboration between people who would not normally come together (networking), and additionally there may be conversations about how to solve common problems (discussion).

Benefits

Holding an event or meeting should provide benefits both for the participants and the organisation. These benefits may be the same for both parties, but may not always be tangible.

They can usually be worked out from the event's purpose(s). For instance, using the special interest group example from the previous section, the expected benefits could be described as follows:

- **Benefits for the participants:** feeling valued as members of the community; a deeper understanding of the subject or issues; making connections with others.
- **Benefits for the organisation:** improved visibility of the organisation; improved reputation as an expert in the field; making connections with others.

You'll notice from the list that some of the benefits are quantifiable, such as "making connections with others"; whilst others are intangible, such as "feeling valued as members of the community". Depending on the purpose of the event, both types may be of equal importance.

Work out the anticipated benefits, how you will capture the data, and what you plan to do with it. For example, if one of the benefits is to gain feedback on a new product or service, you'll need to record that information, perhaps by taking notes (written, audio, or audio-visual) or asking delegates to complete a survey or questionnaire. Improvements to the product or service may then be made based on the collated feedback.

Audience

An event's purpose and benefits will define the type and size of its audience.

Type of audience

If the event is closed (internal to your organisation) or by invitation only, such as a working group or staff training day, you may already have a bank of potential delegates. However, if it's open or you don't have a guest list, you'll have to find your audience.

In both cases, think about inviting colleagues, business associates, and other interested parties. For example, if you're organising a project start-up meeting that all project partners must attend, consider inviting funders, relevant colleagues, and project consultants.

Size of audience

The size of the audience will be limited by factors such as budget, event purpose, and location. Although it may be difficult at this stage to establish an exact number, make an educated guess by thinking about who will benefit from attending.

The event type will also dictate the audience size. For example, a multi-themed conference will consist of more people than a workshop or code bash.

Estimating delegate numbers isn't an exact science. If the event is closed, such as an internal company strategy meeting, you'll probably have a good idea of the audience size. However, it can be harder to estimate attendance if the event is being advertised to the general public and subsequently, whether it is likely to be under-subscribed or over-subscribed.

When attempting to predict the number of potential delegates, include:

- anyone assisting at the event
- colleagues
- consultants
- delegates who choose to attend, such as the general public
- delegates who must attend, such as project staff
- funders
- speakers

> **Tip:** There will be some trial and error in the beginning, particularly if this is your first event. However, it's better to have too many people sign up than not enough because an additional event can always be held at a later date.

Duration

The duration of an event will be determined by its purpose and benefits, and limited by its budget and size or type of audience.

For example, if the purpose of an event is networking, this can be encouraged by including an overnight stay the night before or by splitting the meeting over two half-days, with a conference dinner and accommodation in between. If the focus is on dissemination, fact-finding or discussion, then a half-day or one-day event may be sufficient. However, depending on your budget, an overnight stay may be out of the question.

Similarly, if more than one event is to be held over a period of time (such as a seminar or workshop series) and many of the same people are expected to attend, a half-day or one-day event will be less time-consuming for delegates.

Geographical location

You may already have a region, city, or venue in mind, such as your company's offices. However, if you aren't sure which part of the country (or world) to select, an easy option is to use a location or venue that you have visited before. Otherwise, think about where most of the audience is located. For example, if many of the potential delegates are located in the south-east region of the country, consider finding a venue in that area. This will reduce travelling costs and people may be more willing to attend.

If an overnight stay is a requirement, then consider looking for a location that may be a little further afield. This widens the choice of area because if people have to stay overnight, they may also be more willing to travel further.

If it's proving difficult to settle on a geographic region, choose the selfish option because if running an event on your own, you are responsible for making it happen. Therefore, you need to be at the venue with plenty of time to spare. The safest approach is to stay near or at the venue the night before so you could, in theory, select any location that takes your fancy. However, if you're travelling to the venue on the actual day of the event by car or public transport, find somewhere that is no more than an hour away. Car trouble, transport system malfunctions, or inclement weather are the last things you need when you have sole charge of over fifty delegates.

Once the geographical region has been chosen, think about how the majority of delegates are likely to travel to the event. The meeting location should be easily accessible by public transport: bus, plane, train, tram, or underground/subway.

If most people are flying in, aim for an area within a 15-30 minute bus/tram, taxi, or train/underground ride from the airport.

If delegates are arriving by train, select a location that isn't too far from a major terminus or junction and within a 10-minute walk or public transport/taxi ride from the nearest station.

Ensure that delegates don't have to make too many different connections, because any delays on the public transport system will affect the agenda and people's stress levels. After a long journey with delays, the last thing someone needs is another thirty minutes jammed in a crowded underground train. In any case, if the venue is some distance from the station or airport, people have a tendency to sneak off early to ensure they will catch their main train or flight home.

For larger events, a shuttle bus or pre-booked coach or minibus service can be an option, particularly if most delegates are arriving at a public transport hub at approximately the same time. It also provides some control over when delegates arrive and leave, and can potentially relieve travel stress.

That being said, it is possible to select a location in one of the further outposts of the country, as long as allowance is made in the timing of the agenda. For example, I once held an event in a town that had limited trains to the nearest major city. I simply scheduled the event to start thirty minutes after the arrival of the morning train and to finish thirty minutes before the departure of the afternoon train so people were happy to travel that little bit further.

The design brief gives you clarity and focus by defining the initial requirements. The next stage is to develop a framework for the event by using the brief to create a draft agenda.

Design brief checklist

Time to complete: 15-30 minutes.

Aim: Identify the purpose of the event; benefits for the audience and your organisation; composition and size of the audience; and duration and location of the event.

Purpose
- What is the overall purpose for holding the event?
- What other aims or purposes are there?

Benefits
- What are the tangible and intangible benefits for the audience and for your organisation?
- How will you capture such benefits and what will you do with that information?

Type of audience
- Who is the event for?
- Will it be public or private? By invitation only or open to anyone?
- Do you have a list of potential delegates?
- Do you need to extend the invitation to a wider audience? If so, do you know where to find people who will be interested in attending?

Size of audience
- How many people are expected to attend?

Duration
- How long will the event last?

Geographical location

- Do you have a location or venue in mind? Is there somewhere you've visited before that would be suitable? Otherwise, think about where most of the delegates are located geographically or choose a location close to you.

Chapter 5

Draft Agenda

Drawing up the draft agenda is one of the most creative parts of the *Prepare to Meet* process. At this stage it is simply an outline of the elements necessary to fulfil the design brief, such as the event's title, start and finish times, and Cornerstone and Plug-in Sessions.

The checklist at the end of the chapter will help you formulate the draft agenda. You can then use this to identify staffing and speaker requirements. Don't worry if you don't have all the details to hand, as changes can be made at any part of the planning stage.

Title

It always helps to give an event a name, even if it's only a working title. There are no hard and fast rules other than try to be concise as well as descriptive. However, as Shakespeare says, "a rose by any other name would smell as sweet", so don't spend too long trying to think up a snappy title and keep the event's purpose in mind.

> **Tip:** Include the subject area, target audience, and/or event type as part of the title. For example: "Orthopaedic Consultants' Study Day", "STAR Project Start-up Meeting" or "Moodle Developer Code Bash".

Start and finish times

The start and finish times define the boundaries of the event. They should be sensible and within your industry's standard working hours, unless holding a breakfast meeting or after-work event.

Set the start and finish times so that delegates have time to get to the venue from the nearest major public transport hub and back again before the last bus, plane, train, or tram leaves.

> **Tip:** Even if you don't have a specific location or venue in mind at this stage, make an educated guess at a rough start and finish time. Timings will be subject to change as other elements fall into place.

Parallel strands

Not all events need them, but parallel strands (where sessions run concurrently according to a theme or subset of the audience) are a good way of fitting a lot into a short space of time. For example, a one-day mini-conference on education could be split into separate strands focussing on the technical, pedagogical, and administrative aspects. In this way, one event can cater to several slightly different audiences.

The number of delegates allowed per strand can either be limited according to room capacity or alternatively, meeting rooms can be booked according to the popularity of each strand.

There will always be one or two people who change their mind at the last minute, which isn't a problem. However, if no-one signs up for a particular strand or parallel session, you will need to rethink the agenda.

> **Tip:** Ask delegates to choose their preferred strand in advance so you know what resources (such as size of meeting room or workshop materials) to provide.

Session types

Once the estimated start and finish times are in place, the space between them can be filled with the sessions necessary for fulfilling the design brief. This is the creative part of the process!

There are three types of sessions:

- **Cornerstone:** essential sessions, such as Registration, Welcome, Breaks, and Closing that act as the foundations on which everything else can be built.
- **Plug-in:** these sessions form the substance of the event; such as discussions, presentations, and workshops.
- **Additional:** sessions that are not an integral part of the meeting but which may enhance it, such as conference dinner, entertainment, and pre-conference workshops.

An event will consist of a variety of session types, depending on its purpose and benefits. Here is a list of some of the more common session types:

Cornerstone Sessions

Registration
- Delegates, speakers, and staff are checked off against the delegate list.
- People collect badges, documentation, and other items essential for the event.
- Staff members are on hand to answer any queries.

- See **Registration** (p.28) for more details.
- **Duration:** 20-30 minutes.

Welcome
- Formal opening by the host, sponsor, or company organising the event.
- Housekeeping notices.
- Brief outline of the event.
- Other notices.
- See **Welcome** (p.29) for more details.
- **Duration:** around 10-15 minutes, but may be longer.

Breaks
- **Changeovers:** time for people to move from one room to another; can be used as a comfort break; allow 5 minutes.
- **Coffee/tea breaks:** generally some form of beverage served with a snack; around 10-30 minutes long.
- **Comfort breaks:** where delegates move around, use the bathroom, or get some fresh air; do not usually include refreshments; around 5-10 minutes long.
- **Lunch:** includes food and some form of beverage; around 20-60 minutes long.
- See **Breaks** (p.30) for more details.

Closing
- Brief summary of the event.
- Housekeeping notices.
- Other notices.
- Thank speakers and delegates for attending.
- Wish everyone a safe journey home.
- See **Closing** (p.31) for more details.
- **Duration:** around 10-15 minutes.

Plug-in Sessions

Closed working group (good for: discussion, networking)
- A smaller subset of the audience brainstorms or discusses specific issues, provides progress reports, and sets goals.
- Treat as a mini-event with its own agenda.
- **Duration:** from an hour to a full day.

Code bash (good for: discovery, networking)
- Practical session, similar to a workshop, where software programmers test an aspect of code or share coding tips.
- **Duration:** minimum of an hour; generally a half or full day.

Demonstration (good for: discovery, discussion, dissemination)
- Usually consists of a short presentation, demonstration, and question and answer session.
- **Duration:** 30-90 minutes.

Discussion (good for: discovery, discussion)
- Managed by a facilitator.
- Whole audience takes part either on a specific topic (notified to delegates previously or on the day) or on a topic of the audience's choosing.
- Parallel strands can be used to run several different discussion sessions at the same time.
- See also **Emergency sessions** (p.68).
- **Duration:** from 30 minutes.

Focus group (good for: discovery, discussion)
- Managed by a facilitator.
- Facilitator talks about or demonstrates a specific topic, issue, or product and asks the audience for feedback.
- **Duration:** from 60 minutes to a half or full day.

Icebreaker (good for: networking)
- A light-hearted problem-solving exercise that helps people bond as a group.
- **Duration:** 10-30 minutes.

Keynote (good for: dissemination)
- Sets the tone of the event.
- Delivered by an expert/celebrity in the field or an executive in the organisation.
- **Duration:** 30-45 minutes.

Open mike/show and tell (good for: discovery, dissemination)
- Managed by a facilitator.
- Audience members have a set time limit (usually 5 minutes) to talk about relevant issues (notified to the facilitator in advance or on the day).
- Sometimes followed by a 5 minute question and answer session per speaker.
- See also **Emergency sessions** (p.68).
- **Duration:** 30-90 minutes in total.

Panel session (good for: discussion, dissemination)
- A panel of speakers from the event or other experts answer questions about a specific topic or issue.
- See also **Emergency sessions** (p.68).
- **Duration:** 30-90 minutes.

Presentation (good for: discovery, discussion, dissemination)
- The most common session style; invited speakers present their findings to the audience, using technology, flip-charts, videos, or role-play.
- May also include a question and answer session.
- **Duration:** 20-60 minutes.

Speed networking (good for: dissemination, networking)
- Similar to speed dating; delegates pitch their project/work/idea to other delegates on a one-to-one basis within 3 minutes.
- **Duration:** 30-60 minutes.

Workshop (good for: discovery, dissemination, networking)
- Practical session, often consisting of a short presentation followed by a practical exercise, and follow-up by the facilitator.
- **Duration:** a minimum of an hour, generally two hours or above.

Additional Sessions

Conference dinner (good for: networking)
- Usually a sit-down restaurant-style meal; may also take the form of a buffet.
- May include pre-dinner drinks.
- Often scheduled for around 7pm (give or take half an hour).
- See **Conference dinner** (p.32) for more details.

Entertainment (good for: networking)
- See **After-dinner entertainment** (p.33) for more details.

Overnight stay (good for: networking)
- See **Overnight stay** (p.33) for more details.

Pre-conference workshops
- Treat as a mini-event with its own agenda.
- Usually held as an optional extra on the day before the main event.
- Often practical, such as code bashes or workshops, but may also include product launches or demonstrations.
- **Duration:** usually a half or full-day.

If the purpose of the event is dissemination, it can be easy to fall into the trap of filling the agenda solely with presentation sessions, which can result in audience lethargy and disinterest. Avoid this by asking speakers to be creative and suggest they use flip charts, humour, role play, videos, etc.

If a large number of sessions must be crammed into a short space of time, include something that encourages people to move around, even if it just involves changing seats or taking a comfort break. Any session that involves movement, interaction (such as talking or laughing), or a change of pace will result in people remembering the event because they are actively engaged in the subject matter.

Make sure the event is focussed on the main topic area rather than trying to cast the net too wide. Sessions that centre around the purpose of the event will make it more memorable and beneficial. However, the occasional wildcard topic can provide variety as well as being a creative way to fill the odd gap in the agenda.

> **Tip:** Avoid filling the agenda with nothing but PowerPoint presentations, as people tend to lose concentration after a while. Instead, keep the audience engaged by interspersing presentations with something more interactive, such as practical or discussion sessions.

Registration

Most people will arrive during the Registration session, although one or two will always arrive up to an hour earlier or later. Thirty minutes is usually long enough for delegates to pick up badges and documentation, ask any questions, and grab a coffee.

If the event is being held over two days and additional delegates are expected on the second day, schedule a Registration session for each day.

> **Tip:** If extra sessions need to be squeezed into the agenda, the Registration session can be shortened by up to ten minutes.

Welcome

The Welcome session sets the scene. It often starts with a formal opening by a representative from the company running the event or by someone from a different organisation acting as the host or sponsor.

Housekeeping announcements should also be made during this session either by the person opening the event or some other nominated person. Housekeeping announcements should cover:

- emergency evacuation instructions
- location of emergency exits
- notification of any fire alarm tests
- location of toilets
- catering arrangements
- access to Wi-Fi and password
- return of badges, documentation, or other equipment
- logistics for any parallel strands
- expected finish time
- any other notices

A brief overview of the event can be included in the Welcome session, but it can also be scheduled as a separate session after the housekeeping announcements. Use it to outline the agenda and event purpose, and to describe some of the anticipated benefits.

The Welcome session should last around ten to fifteen minutes. If this isn't long enough, perhaps because the event's context requires a more detailed explanation, schedule it as a separate session. This will help the audience to get a better sense of the event's purpose and logical progression. It can also provide the opportunity for an additional presentation should you be struggling to fill the agenda.

If the event is being held over more than one day, schedule a very short Welcome session for each day. Around five minutes should be ample. On subsequent days this can be an excellent opportunity to address any logistical issues or changes.

> **Tip:** If extra sessions need to be squeezed into the agenda, the Welcome session can be shortened by around five minutes.

Breaks

Breaks are an important and integral part of any meeting because they provide people with the opportunity to move around, network, and get some fresh air.

Modify the length of the breaks according to the design brief. For example, if the event's main purpose is to encourage networking, opt for longer breaks. If it is fact-finding or dissemination, make the breaks shorter. Schedule a break approximately every two hours. Even if the session is a three-hour workshop, make time for a short break.

There are several different types of break, including:

- **Changeovers:** If people have to move from one room to another, the changeover gives everyone time to get to the next session. This time can also be used as a comfort break. **Duration:** Allow around five minutes for the changeover.
- **Coffee/tea breaks:** These breaks are a good opportunity for people to network and discuss the previous session(s). Usually, one is scheduled for mid-morning and one for mid-afternoon. Some form of beverage and snack (such as a biscuit, cake, or fruit platter) is usually offered. **Duration:** 15-30 minutes each.
- **Comfort breaks:** If people have to sit in one place for a full two hours, a comfort break gives people the opportunity to use the bathroom, get some fresh air, or stretch their legs. Refreshments are not usually provided, unless they are supplied by machine or are

supplemental to the main refreshment breaks. These breaks do not necessarily have to be scheduled into the agenda. **Duration:** approximately 5-10 minutes.
- **Lunch:** Lunch can be a sit-down restaurant-style meal, self-service buffet, or simply a selection of sandwiches from the local shop. It may be provided by the venue, external caterers, or the organiser (in the case of purchased sandwiches). In some cases, delegates may even be asked to provide their own lunch. Some form of beverage is usually offered. Most day and overnight delegate rates include one lunch as standard. If the event runs over two half-days with an overnight stay, decide on which day(s) lunch is required. **Duration:** Depending on the event's purpose, anywhere from 20 to 60 minutes.

> **Tip:** As the agenda timings are refined throughout this process, the elastic quality of breaks can be exploited. In other words, if extra sessions need to be squeezed into the agenda, the breaks can be shortened. Conversely, if you have a little more time available, the length of the breaks can be extended.

Closing

The Closing session concludes the event and usually lasts around ten to fifteen minutes. It is used to:

- express appreciation to speakers and colleagues
- thank delegates for attending
- provide a brief summary of the event
- remind delegates about any housekeeping procedures, such as returning visitor passes
- announce any notices, such as future events and reminders to fill in the follow-up survey
- wish everyone a safe journey home

If the event is being held over more than one day, schedule a very short Closing session for each day, summarising the day's events and reminding delegates of the next day's schedule. Around five minutes should be ample.

> **Tip:** Again, if an extra presentation needs to be inserted into the agenda, this session can be reduced by five minutes or so.

Conference dinner

If delegates are required to stay overnight during any part of the event, an evening meal (conference dinner) should be provided.

A conference dinner generally takes the form of a sit-down restaurant-style meal, although a self-service buffet-style approach may also be taken. Each venue (or restaurant) has their own way of catering for large numbers of people. Here are just a few of the options:

- A set menu where each course is pre-chosen by the organiser.
- A set menu with limited choices from which delegates may choose.
- An à la carte menu from which delegates may choose any dish.
- Delegates pre-book their menu choice on registering to attend the event.

The conference dinner may be held at the venue or at a nearby restaurant. In both cases, the venue or restaurant should be able to seat the anticipated number of people, preferably all in the same room. I attended one conference where a dozen of us had to eat in a separate part of the building away from the main dining area because the venue did not have enough space for everyone to sit together. This made us feel rather left out.

> **Tip:** Include dining arrangements in the pre-event information so that delegates know what to expect.

After-dinner entertainment

A conference dinner and access to a bar or pub is usually sufficient to encourage networking. However, other activities such as a pub quiz, wine-tasting, or other entertainment may be offered.

Avoid scheduling additional working events after dinner because as the day wears on delegates get tired and just want to relax. However, be prepared for networking to continue well after the bar has closed and for some bleary-eyed delegates in the morning. Wise delegates and organisers will get an early night!

Overnight stay

The main reasons for offering an overnight stay (regardless of who is paying) are to encourage networking or collaboration, and to provide ease of access to the event.

At this stage, you should know whether an overnight stay is a fundamental part of the event. If it is, then consider whether delegates should stay at the venue itself or in accommodation nearby.

Using the venue's accommodation can intensify the networking process as people bump into each other in corridors and other public spaces. The environment soon becomes familiar and people will seek out places for impromptu meetings. If your party is the only one using the venue, the intimacy of the event can make delegates feel more relaxed. However, there is a danger that people can get a bit stir crazy if they have to eat, sleep, and work in the same place for more than a couple of days!

If people are staying outside of the venue, networking often occurs on the walk between the conference centre and the hotel, although this may not be as intense, bearing in mind the small window of opportunity for this to take place. Accommodating people outside of the venue's confines can be beneficial for events longer than a couple of days so that people can have a change of scene and time alone to recharge and relax.

> **Tip:** Don't forget to think about accommodation for staff members and/or speakers should they need to travel a long way or be briefed the night before.

Drafting the agenda

Once the Cornerstone Sessions of Registration, Welcome, Breaks, and Closing are in place, arrange the other elements around them. You may already have some idea of the titles, topics, or potential speakers for each session. If so, pencil them in. Otherwise, add a placeholder identifying what you want to happen and when.

Delegates sometimes sneak away during the mid-afternoon tea break, so hold the most important sessions mid-way through the event when the largest portion of the audience is present. Schedule any star speakers straight after the Welcome or Keynote sessions.

Make sure any sessions that don't require audience participation or engagement are no longer than 45 minutes, because energy levels start to flag when people have to sit still for too long. Avoid "death by PowerPoint" by interspersing static presentations with activities or sessions that require interaction or movement.

> **Tip:** Don't forget to add timings for sessions that take place outside of the main event; such as the conference dinner, bar opening/closing times, after-dinner entertainment, breakfast, etc.

Draft agenda examples

Here are a couple of draft agenda examples. The Cornerstone sessions are in bold and marked with an asterisk (*) so that you can see how they act as a foundation on which the rest of the event is built.

Example 1: One day single strand event
Purpose: discovery, discussion, and dissemination

09:00 Registration and refreshments*
09:20 Welcome*
09:30 Presentations
10:30 Demonstration
10:45 Coffee break*
11:00 Presentations
12:30 Lunch*
13:15 Workshop
15:00 Tea break*
15:15 Presentation
15:45 Discussion
16:30 Closing*
16:45 End of event*

Example 2: Event held over two half days with parallel strands, conference dinner, and overnight accommodation
Purpose: dissemination and networking

Day 1
13:00 Lunch for staff*
14:00 Registration and refreshments*
14:20 Welcome*
14:30 Keynote
15:00 Icebreaker

15:30 Presentations
16:00 Tea break*
16:30 Parallel strands (one for Group 1 projects; one for Group 2 projects)
17:55 Closing (within parallel strands)*
18:00 End of Day 1*
19:00 Conference dinner and bar

Day 2

Note that an additional Registration session is not required because no additional delegates are expected on the second day.

07:30 Breakfast*
08:45 Welcome*
08:50 Workshop
11:00 Coffee break*
11:30 Demonstration
12:00 Presentations
12:45 Closing*
13:00 Lunch*
14:00 End of Day 2*

The draft agenda can be thought of as an artist's impression of the event as a whole. Of course, it will change over time as each element drops into place. For now, it is simply a rough-and-ready structure on which to build the next part of the process: the people.

Draft agenda checklist

Time to complete: One to two hours.

Aim: Draw up the draft agenda based on the design brief by giving the event a name, specifying the start and finish times, and identifying the session types.

Title
- Devise a concise and descriptive title.

Start and finish times
- Specify the start and finish times for each day.

Parallel strands
- If running parallel sessions or strands, do they run through all or part of the event? What are the themes?

Drafting the agenda
- Establish the Cornerstone sessions for each day.
- If the event runs over two half-days, on which days is lunch required?
- Identify the Plug-in and Additional sessions.

Conference dinner
- If delegates are staying overnight, on which evenings should a conference dinner be provided? Where will it be held?

Entertainment
- Do you need access to a bar or pub or to arrange after-dinner entertainment?

Overnight stay
- Are delegates, staff, and/or speakers required to stay overnight? If so, when and where?

Chapter 6

PEOPLE

As Helen Keller says, "Alone we can do so little; together we can do so much." A face-to-face meeting is ideal for bringing together experts and novices, management and staff, businesses and customers. If managed well, hierarchies and boundaries are blurred, relationships are formed, and knowledge is expanded.

This chapter will help you to identify who will deliver the sessions outlined in the draft agenda (speakers/experts); establish who will lend a hand with the organisation, facilitation, and running of the event (assistants/staff); and to work out the guest list (delegates/customers).

Speakers

Unless you are running every session by yourself, you will need to find one or more speakers. You may already have potential candidates in mind. If not, consider adding colleagues, funders, or others with whom you already have a relationship to the speaker list.

If you're struggling to find speakers, here are a few suggestions:

- advertise on your event website
- ask colleagues or associates for recommendations
- contact experts in your industry
- read journals, magazines, and blogs

- look at similar events for speakers in same field, but ensure they give a different presentation (unless your audience won't have heard it before)
- search the internet and use social media

Draw up a list of speakers that is longer than actually required because people may not be available on the date of the event. Put potential speakers in order of preference. Those at the bottom of the list can be held in reserve. If people are not available on this occasion, consider asking them to present at a later event.

> **Tip:** If it is proving difficult to find speakers, schedule a discussion or panel session led by people who have already agreed to present.

Assistants

I know from first-hand experience that it is quite possible to plan, organise, and run an event without any assistance. I have done so on many occasions using the process in this book. However, it is always a good idea to get help where you can and whilst it is possible to run an event on your own for up to 80 people, I recommend enlisting at least one assistant for each additional batch of 80 delegates.

There are a number of roles that can be assigned to an additional member of staff or split up amongst colleagues. Decide who will:

- have **ultimate responsibility** should it all go horribly wrong (in other words, whose head will be on the chopping block?)
- be designated as **chief organiser** (this is likely to be you)
- be responsible for **budget issues and finance**
- help with any of the **organisation or planning** aspects
- provide **administration or secretarial assistance**, such as printing, advertising, badges, and documentation preparation
- assist on the day of the event (see below)

If you are planning and organising the event on your own, you will perform almost all of those roles. However, if you're fortunate enough to have assistance from colleagues, decide who will do what and when during the planning and organisation stages based on their skill sets and compatibility. For larger events with multiple organisers and assistants, consider drawing up a code of conduct and list of expectations so that each party clearly understands their role.

If colleagues are available to help during the actual event, identify who will:

- **attend as an assistant** and define their role
- **bring components**, such as workshop materials, laptop, documentation, or badges
- **liaise with the venue, catering team, or technicians** in case of problems
- **staff the registration desk** and welcome delegates
- **facilitate the event** on the day (act as compère)
- **take notes** during the event

> **Tip:** Don't forget that you will need someone to facilitate any parallel strands or sessions on the day. A good rule of thumb is to have at least one colleague per strand or session.

Audience

You may already have a guest list or a ready-made audience, particularly if the meeting is closed or by invitation only, such as a staff training workshop. Otherwise, you will need to promote the event. If so, think about advertising on:

- industry or subject-specific forums, mailing lists, or magazines
- posters
- social media

- word of mouth
- your organisation's website

Depending on the event's purpose and intended audience, consider inviting people with whom you already have a relationship, such as:

- business associates
- business partners
- colleagues
- consultants
- funders
- project staff
- sponsors

Unless the event is closed and it is mandatory for people to attend (such as a staff meeting), put more people on the guest list than the budget or venue capacity will allow. Numbers can always be limited as people sign up. In any case, not everyone will register to attend and of those that do, not everyone will actually turn up.

> **Tip:** Don't forget to include speakers and assistants, when drawing up the delegate list.

Now that potential speakers, assistants, and delegates have been identified, the next step is to draw up the venue brief.

People checklist

Time to complete: 20-60 minutes.

Aim: Identify who will deliver each session (speakers), help with the event (assistants), and attend (delegates).

Speakers
- Do you have a list of potential speakers? If so, for which sessions?
- If not, where will you find speakers?

Assistants: planning and organising stages
- Who will have ultimate responsibility for the event?
- Who is the chief organiser?
- Who is responsible for budget issues and finance?
- Who will assist with the organisation or planning aspects and what will they do?
- Who will provide administration or secretarial assistance?

Assistants: on the day
- Who will assist you and what will they do?
- Who will bring any materials?
- In case of problems, who will liaise with the venue, catering team, or technicians?
- Who will staff the registration desk, facilitate the event on the day, take notes, and run any parallel strands or sessions?

Audience
- Do you have a list of potential delegates?
- If not, how will you find your audience? Do you need to advertise the event? If so, where?

Chapter 7

VENUE BRIEF

Taking time out now to draft the venue brief will make life easier during the organising stage because you will have all the information at your fingertips. However, there's no need to look for a venue just yet, as we are still at the planning stage.

This brief sets out the date or timescale for the event, and the venue requirements in terms of room size, furniture, and refreshments.

At this point, the brief simply specifies the primary requirements necessary for booking a venue. Secondary requirements, such as audio-visual equipment, may not be immediately obvious, but can be arranged during the organising stage.

Space requirements

The most important element is to define the functional space that will fulfil the requirements laid out in the design brief and draft agenda. Meeting rooms should be large enough to accommodate each session's audience, from keynote to conference dinner and everything in between.

The main conference room must be able to seat all attendees, as should any restaurant space. Breakout/syndicate rooms should be large enough to accommodate everyone involved in the parallel session (including speakers and assistants) being held there. Some spaces can fulfil several functions: for example, the main conference room can be used for meeting, dining, and entertaining.

Here are some common functional space requirements:

- **Main conference room:** must be large enough to accommodate all the delegates at once; can also be used for larger parallel sessions.
- **Breakout/syndicate room(s):** dependent on the number of parallel strands and type of sessions being offered. Factor in the main conference room when working out the number of breakout rooms required. For example, if there are three parallel strands, you will need the main conference room plus two breakout rooms.
- **Registration table:** usually placed just outside or inside the main conference room; may occasionally be in a different room or location.
- **Refreshments:** determined by the venue's facilities, and the event's catering needs (sit-down meal or buffet, and beverages). Location may be dictated by the venue. Refreshments may be served in: the main conference room, the venue's restaurant, a public space outside the main room, or in a separate room.
- **Conference dinner (optional):** determined by the venue's facilities, and your menu choice (restaurant style or buffet), and whether delegates are required to stay overnight. If the venue is not providing the conference dinner, find a restaurant or caterer who can offer this service.
- **Entertainment space (optional):** depending on the entertainment being offered, it may be possible to use the venue's bar or the main conference room. Otherwise, you will need to book a separate room or find an additional venue that can offer the necessary service.
- **Bar (optional):** access to a bar (or pub) for networking if delegates are required to stay overnight.
- **Accommodation (optional):** provision or access to accommodation if delegates are required to stay overnight. This may be located within or outside the venue.

> **Tip:** If finances are limited, hold two simultaneous discussions in the main conference room instead of booking a breakout room. Similarly, if discussion groups are small and quiet, it may be possible to use the venue's public space, but don't rely on it being available if other events are being held in the same building.

Room layout

Once the overall space requirements have been defined, the next step is to specify the layout for each room, according to its main function.

Most venues provide a chart showing the dimensions of each meeting room and the maximum number of delegates that can be accommodated depending on the arrangement of the furniture (tables and chairs).

Bear in mind that different room layouts will affect the number of delegates that can be seated. Generally, the more furniture there is in a room, the fewer delegates can be accommodated.

Layouts are generally as follows:

- **Boardroom style:** one large or several smaller tables put together in a rectangular shape with chairs around the sides and ends (may seat up to 20 people)
- **Cabaret style:** separate tables usually accommodating 6-10 people with chairs all around; ideal for practical and discussion sessions (may seat over 100 people)
- **Classroom style:** rows of tables with chairs facing the front; useful for practical sessions where people need to write or use computers (may seat less than 100 people)
- **Theatre style:** chairs in rows facing the front (no tables); perfect for the main conference room and presentation-style sessions (may seat over 100 people)
- **U-shape:** tables laid out in a U-shape, with chairs around the outside and occasionally on the inside (may seat up to 25 people).

Tables are usually essential for workshops or other practical sessions; therefore consider selecting a cabaret or classroom style layout (depending on the audience size). For discussions, choose boardroom style, cabaret style, classroom style, or U-shape.

If the main conference room also doubles as a room for a session requiring tables, then opt for a cabaret or classroom style layout for the whole day because it will be impracticable to move furniture around between sessions.

Regardless of room layout, a registration table is essential. This is usually located just outside or inside the main conference room, although it may occasionally be placed in a separate room (or even a different part of the building). The venue should supply this as part of the contract, but request one anyway.

> **Tip:** Always ask for an extra table just inside the main conference room because it will serve a number of purposes. For example, it can act as a registration table for late arrivals, and for displaying brochures or other documentation for collection by delegates. Badges or other equipment can be dropped off there as everyone leaves. Plus, it is a handy place for people to deposit any crockery or rubbish, which will save time when you clear up at the end of the day.

Refreshments

As a general rule of thumb, refreshments should be offered:

- on arrival/at registration
- at mid-morning
- with lunch
- at mid-afternoon (optional, depending on the event's finish time)

Delegate rates usually include refreshments at most, if not all, of those times. However, some venues are more generous than others.

A day delegate rate is a package provided by the venue usually consisting of room hire, refreshments (beverages and lunch), and flip chart. An overnight delegate rate additionally includes conference dinner, and bed and breakfast accommodation.

Include non-caffeinated drinks, such as herbal tea, water, and/or fruit juice in the venue brief for those who do not drink coffee or tea. Most venues supply a range of beverages at break times and a sweet snack, such as a pastry or cake, during coffee/tea breaks as part of the delegate rate. Some venues may offer a fruit platter (this may cost extra), which is a more refreshing option that reduces the late-morning and afternoon sugar crash.

If booking beverages separately (either outside of the delegate rate or when using your company meeting rooms), make sure there are sufficient hot drinks for everyone, and enough tap or bottled water for about half the delegates. A one litre bottle of water should serve around 6-8 individuals. People also like to nibble on something with their coffee/tea, so if you're counting the pennies order or bring in a plate of biscuits, even if you can only afford one biscuit each. I have been to several events where some people were left thirsty because insufficient beverages had been ordered. This did not set a good tone for the rest of the event.

Include requirements for any additional refreshments if the event is being run over two half days or includes an overnight stay, such as:

- an additional lunch (for all delegates or for staff only)
- conference dinner
- access to a bar (or pub)
- breakfast

> **Tip:** If using external caterers to provide refreshments or a hotel outside the venue to provide accommodation, split the venue brief into different sections detailing what is required from each supplier and when.

Date

You may already know when to hold your event: for example, at the beginning of a new project or on completion of a company milestone. Sometimes, a meeting can be run back-to-back with another in the same subject area. However, if you don't have a specific date, start by choosing a month and work out everything else from that point.

When selecting dates, ensure that no other conferences in the same subject area are scheduled to take place within a couple of weeks of that timeframe. For example, one department I worked in held a two-day conference every year, for which funding had to be negotiated, so it could take time for the arrangements to be confirmed. One year, the money took longer than usual to come through, so the organisers hastily selected a date. It was only after invitations had been sent out that they realised the leading industry conference was scheduled for exactly the same date. This meant backtracking on everything and starting again.

Therefore, always check what external and internal meetings are scheduled so that your event reaches the largest potential audience. Take into account any staff appraisals or other major company occasions that could have an impact on the choice of date.

On the other hand, there is no guarantee that a major event won't suddenly pop up out of the blue. For example, I once booked a two-day project wind-up event four months ahead. I did all my homework, checked the calendars, and found nothing relevant on the horizon. One month later, with all the details in place, a leading player suddenly announced the dates for their conference, which was going to run one day into my event.

It was mandatory for people to attend this meeting as a condition of their funding, and because the venue booking, agenda, and speakers had all been finalised, I decided to continue. There were a couple of complaints, but not everyone was going to attend the major conference anyway and those that did only lost one day of a three-day event. If this happens to you, weigh up whether it is worthwhile continuing with your preferred date or changing the date based on: how much has already been organised, any funding implications, and the potential effects of a more prestigious event being held at the same time.

Drawing up a design brief, draft agenda, and venue brief provides a structure for an event in almost no time. Most of the major decisions are made early in the process, and this makes life much easier when you get to the organising stage. However, before we jump ahead, we need to work out how to finance the event.

Venue brief checklist

Time to complete: 20-60 minutes.

Aim: Set the date and use the venue brief to detail the venue requirements, such as room size, furniture and refreshments.

Space requirements and room layout
- **Main conference room:** How many delegates does it need to hold? What layout do you need?
- **Breakout/syndicate rooms:** How many do you need and for what capacity? What layout do you need?
- **Registration table:** Do you have any special location requirements?
- **Refreshments:** Do you have any special requirements for where or how refreshments should be served?
- **Conference dinner (optional):** Who will provide dinner? Are there any special requirements for where or how it should be served?
- **Entertainment (optional):** What do you need? Are there any special requirements?
- **Bar (optional):** What do you need? Who will provide the bar service?
- **Accommodation (optional):** Where do you expect delegates to stay?

Refreshments
- What refreshments are required and when? Who will provide them?
- Do you have any additional or special catering requirements? When do you need them?

Date
- Does the event need to be held at a specific time? If not, do you have a rough timescale?

- When are your industry's major conferences scheduled?
- Are there any events taking place within your organisation that should be taken into account?

Chapter 8

BUDGET

The lists of requirements drawn up in the design and venue briefs should give you a rough idea of costs. For example, a half-day event held at your company's offices will cost much less than a two-day conference at a prestigious hotel. Depending on how the event will be financed, you may need to ask delegates to subsidise the event.

This chapter will help you decide whether to charge an attendance fee, and how to spend the budget. At this stage, you don't need to allocate every penny; simply prioritise your requirements based on the design brief, draft agenda, and venue brief.

Attendance fees

The first step is to establish how much money is available to pay for the event. Some organisations are fortunate enough to have funds available as part of their company strategy or a sponsor or funder may finance meetings as part of a project plan. If the event is fully financed, it may be free for delegates to attend as a stipulation of the funding, for example.

It is not always necessary to have a pot of money available to finance an event for external delegates. There are ways and means of making it pay for itself. If internal finances aren't available or are insufficient, then an attendance fee can be charged. Some or all of the costs can be passed on to delegates, such as:

- accommodation
- additional sessions, such as pre-conference workshops
- attending the event itself
- conference dinner and entertainment
- travel expenses (some project budgets include travel expenses for delegates, especially if the event is designed for a closed community)

When calculating an appropriate attendance fee, decide whether to cover your costs, include a charge for overheads or add a profit margin. Options include:

- **Everything is free** and paid for by your organisation, sponsor, or funder.
- **No charge to attend** but delegates pay for conference dinner, additional sessions, overnight accommodation, etc.
- **A fee to cover delegate costs only,** such as day delegate rate, conference dinner, technology hire, accommodation, etc.
- **A fee to cover delegate costs plus overheads** relating to staff time, stationery, workshop materials, staff travel, etc.
- **A fee to cover all costs with an added profit margin**: includes delegate costs (such as day delegate rate), overheads (such as staff time), plus an additional profit margin.

If an overnight stay is required as part of the event, decide whether the attendance fee will include accommodation costs or whether delegates should book (and pay for) their own. If choosing the first option, persuade a colleague to help specifically with this aspect as there will be plenty of time-consuming contact with the hotel or venue.

> **Tip:** If you have limited external funding and require delegates to stay overnight, negotiate a special rate for accommodation with the venue or hotel and ask people to book and pay for it themselves. Not only does this reduce the financial burden, but it also reduces the workload.

Payment

If charging people to attend, decide how you will collect payment and set a deadline for receipt of fees. Options include:

- Receiving **cash payments** at the door: suitable for small events, with extremely low fees.
- Sending each delegate an **invoice**: if done manually, there will be an increased workload and follow-up is required if delegates do not pay on time.
- Taking a **credit card or PayPal payment**: processes should be in place before advertising the event. If your organisation is not set up for this, consider using an online service for collecting payment, providing receipts and refunds, and for transferring and auditing any income from the event.

An easy approach to handling payments and delegate registration is to use an online event ticketing service, such as **EventBrite**[1], which offers a range of functions including: event page customisation, payment choices (such as PayPal, credit card, or debit card), ticket bundles (where delegates pay for different aspects of the event), tracking, refunds, links to social media, etc. Some services can even be used for sending invitations. If the event is free, there is not normally a service charge; otherwise fees usually include a percentage of the ticket price, plus handling fee, plus payment processing fee.

Having thought about delegate attendance fees, consider whether you expect speakers to pay to attend. Some conferences make speakers pay either the full or a reduced price, whilst others waive such fees completely.

---

[1] http://www.eventbrite.co.uk/

> **Tip:** If covering attendance costs for speakers and assistants, and using an online event ticketing service, provide a discount code so that they can register themselves for the event for free or at a lower rate. This will reduce your workload because you won't be responsible for registering them, although you may have to check that they have done so.

Expenditure

Most of the budget will be consumed by costs associated with the venue, such as room hire and refreshments. Other major expenditure may include speaker fees and expenses. Following is a list of items on which to spend your money. This list assumes that the event will be held at a conference venue. However, if holding the event in-house, each item may need to be budgeted for separately. For example, outside caterers may be commissioned to provide lunch, whilst you buy the teabags for the coffee break from petty cash.

At the venue

- **Day delegate rate:** usually includes refreshments, lunch, hire of main conference room, one flip chart, projector and screen (sometimes there is a fee for the technology).
- **Overnight delegate rate:** as per the day delegate rate; also includes conference dinner, accommodation, and breakfast.
- **Negotiated rate:** where you pay for some elements (such as room hire) and delegates pay for others (such as lunch).
- **Accommodation:** additional to that included in the overnight delegate rate.
- **Additional flip charts, provision of stationery, fax and printing services** supplied by the venue.

- **Additional items:** such as extension leads or multiway bar extension sockets (if delegates are required to bring their own laptops). Note: aside from personal devices, if supplying your own electrical equipment the venue may request evidence of PAT (Portable Appliance Testing).
- **Additional refreshments:** served during an extra break or not included in the delegate rates.
- **Breakout/syndicate rooms:** usually include a flip chart; projector and screen hire may be included or may cost extra.
- **Conference dinner:** additional to or not included in an overnight delegate rate.
- **Drinks at dinner:** wine, water, etc. There are approximately six glasses in a standard bottle of wine or litre bottle of water. As a general rule of thumb, provide one bottle of red wine and one of white, plus one bottle of water per table of six.
- **Entertainment:** such as an open bar (where the organiser pays the drinks bill), wine tasting, musical/theatrical entertainment, etc.
- **Technology:** such as Wi-Fi (some venues charge extra), hire of a computer (bring your own laptop to keep costs down) and projector (you could bring your own to keep costs down, but it is worth paying to use the venue's in case of technology failure), any audio-visual equipment (such as microphone and speakers), video-links, technical assistance, etc.

Speaker expenses

- **Fees and expenses:** speaking fees, travel, accommodation, subsistence, delegate fees to attend the event, etc.

Assistant expenses

- **Hire of additional staff:** to assist with any aspect of the event.
- **Expenses:** travel, accommodation, subsistence, overtime, etc. Remember to include your own expenses.

Incidentals

- **Advertising:** depending on the purpose of the event.
- **Contingency fund:** always keep a little aside for the unexpected, such as a sudden request for a videographer or more expensive wine (yes, it does happen and usually at the last minute!).
- **Merchant service or PayPal fees:** if setting up your own ticket purchasing service.
- **Online event ticketing service fees:** usually a percentage of the ticket price, plus handling fee, plus payment processing fee.
- **Printing and stationery:** such as agendas, badges, badge inserts, delegate packs, materials for workshops, etc.

At this stage, simply identify and prioritise everything you need, as you won't necessarily have the exact costs to hand. For example, if funds are limited, find a venue with a cheap delegate rate and reduce the catering costs by choosing a more basic menu option. If you don't have the time or staff resources to deal with the ticketing and payment aspects, use an online event ticketing service and mark it as a priority.

> **Tip:** If you need to save a few pennies at the conference dinner, ask for a carafe of tap water and make two bottles of wine serve a table of eight.

As well as knowing how much money is available to spend on the event, it is also important to be aware of exactly how much remains at any one time. The next step is to work out who will be responsible for keeping track of expenditure.

Budget checklist

Time to complete: 30-60 minutes.

Aim: To work out how much you have to spend and what to spend it on.

Attendance fees
- Do you have a budget and if so, how much? Who is providing the funds?
- Are you charging an attendance fee and if so, what will it cover?
- Will the attendance fee cover the actual costs or do you need to add overheads or a profit margin?
- Are delegates expected to book and pay for their own accommodation? If not, who will handle this aspect?

Payment
- If charging an attendance fee, how will payment be collected? Consider using an online event ticketing service to handle the booking and financial aspects (remember there are associated costs unless the event is free to attend).
- Are the financial processes for handling any income in place?
- If charging an attendance fee, how much will speakers and assistants pay?
- If waiving or reducing fees for speakers/assistants and using an online event ticketing service, remember to provide a discount code.

Expenditure: at the venue
Prioritise each element required:
- accommodation
- additional flip charts, stationery, fax and printing by the venue
- additional items: such as extension leads and multiway bar extension sockets
- additional refreshments

- breakout/syndicate rooms
- conference dinner
- delegate rate: day, overnight, or negotiated
- drinks at dinner
- entertainment
- technology: such as Wi-Fi, computer and projector hire, audio-visual equipment, video-links, and technical assistance

Expenditure: speaker and assistant expenses

Prioritise each element required:
- speaker fees and expenses
- hire of additional staff
- staff expenses

Expenditure: incidentals

Prioritise each element required:
- contingency fund
- merchant service or PayPal fees
- online event ticketing service fees
- printing and stationery

Chapter 9

KEEPING TRACK

Keeping track of payments is an important part of financial management, but you also need to have an overview of your company's financial processes such as purchasing, invoicing, and supplier payment. This chapter will help you identify who is responsible for keeping track of expenditure and making financial decisions, determine how your organisation's financial processes work, and ensure there is access to emergency funds.

Monitoring the budget

No matter how well you plan, the unexpected can happen, so it is important that you know exactly how much money is left to spend on the event at all times. Therefore, someone should be responsible for monitoring the budget. You, as organiser, should take on the role (in addition to someone more senior) so that if any unexpected expenditure arises, you will know immediately whether it is affordable.

For example, the funders for one of our events decided at the last minute that they wanted a more expensive wine served at the conference dinner. However, I could see by keeping track of the finances that the budget wouldn't cover it. The funders agreed to give us a very small additional sum, which still wasn't sufficient to provide the usual bottle of red and bottle of white per table of six. So I asked the venue to make the bottles stretch to a table of eight. This turned out to be ample because there was also a bar at the venue. In any case, as the event was free for delegates to attend, nobody had any cause for complaint!

Negotiating and signing contracts

When liaising with suppliers, there are two roles to consider. The first involves the negotiation of the contact details, whilst the second concerns the responsibility for the financial decisions. Both roles may be fulfilled by the same person (and as organiser, it may well be you) or by two different people. It all depends on the chain of command in your organisation.

In the initial conversation with the venue, speakers, and other suppliers, the contract negotiator will be responsible for arranging a suitable rate for each service. At this point, nothing is signed.

Depending on the level of financial responsibility, you or your superior will then accept the proposed rates and sign the contract. The venue will hold the signatory accountable should the event be cancelled or monies not be received.

It makes life a lot easier if you (as organiser) have responsibility for negotiating rates as well as signing contracts, especially if additional items need to be added at the last minute.

On one occasion, after signing a contract with the venue, we later decided to split one of the sessions into two parallel strands, for which we needed an additional break-out room. Fortunately, there was one available and it was just a case of drawing up a new contract, which had to be signed again. I was able to do this very quickly because I had the appropriate level of authority. Also, as I was monitoring the budget, I knew there was enough money to cover the additional cost. This is why it can be useful to keep some of the budget in a contingency fund.

Tip: Try to ensure that the chain of command is not so complex that it takes weeks to get a signature. Suppliers will usually hold a tentative booking for only two weeks (or less).

Financial processes

Every organisation has its own way of handling financial processes. Whilst you don't need to know all the intricate details, you should have an overview of your company's procedures for purchasing, invoicing, and supplier payment.

Speakers

There are various ways of handling the financial relationship with speakers depending on your organisation's approach.

For example, some companies treat a speaker in the same way as a supplier, adding them to their financial payments system. It may be necessary to draw up a purchase order, authorised by the relevant person, to ensure that the service procured is legitimate and can be traced along the audit trail. If speakers are treated as suppliers, they may be required to provide an invoice with the purchase order, supplier, or other reference number.

Other organisations may treat a speaker as a temporary member of staff, adding them to the Human Resource Department's database as an external contractor. In which case, they may have to complete an internal or external expenses form in order to be paid.

On the other hand, your company's processes may be less formal and a simple letter from the speaker outlining their costs with any attached receipts may be sufficient.

Regardless of whether or not speakers are being paid for their services, you should also have an overview of your organisation's process for speakers claiming additional expenses, such as travel or accommodation. Some organisations may use an expenses claim form, whilst others may ask speakers to add such costs to their invoice along with copies of receipts.

Assistants

You should also understand how the process works for colleagues (assistants) who need to claim for travel, accommodation, or other incidentals. For example, some organisations ask their staff to complete an internal expenses form, whilst others are happy to receive a bunch of receipts. One or two may even give their staff a per diem payment.

Some firms ask staff (and speakers) to book accommodation and travel via a central booking service or travel agent, whilst others allow people to make all the arrangements themselves. A few organisations may ask staff to raise a purchase order to cover travel and/or accommodation costs, especially if it exceeds a certain amount.

Services

It should be easier to determine the financial processes relating to the supply of services, such as the venue, accommodation, or entertainment. Service providers are generally set up as a supplier on your organisation's accounting system and a purchase order raised. They are then provided with a reference number to display on their invoice.

Delegates

Depending on the nature of the event, the budget may cover delegates' travel and/or accommodation costs (if separate from an overnight delegate rate). Therefore, you need to know how your organisation handles such expense claims by external parties.

However, try to avoid increasing the workload of either your company's administrative staff or yourself. For example, I once attended a two-day conference where the funders agreed to pay accommodation costs. Unfortunately, because the organisers didn't know exactly how many bedrooms were needed, they asked delegates to book and pay for their accommodation and then submit an invoice for reimbursement. This resulted in over 150 invoices for the same amount being channelled through one administrative assistant. All of which had to be verified and put on the finance system. She wasn't happy!

Payment methods

As well as having a general idea of the financial paper trail, you also need to know your organisation's method for paying speakers, assistants, and suppliers. Invoices and subsistence claims may be paid via cheque, electronic transfer, or some other mechanism. For example, staff expenses may be refunded during the monthly salary run, whilst speakers are paid by cheque.

Contact

Payments can be delayed for a variety of reasons and a speaker or supplier will usually approach the organiser first. Therefore, find out who to contact in your Accounts Department in case of any queries.

Credit cards

Finally, this is a small but important point: if you're attending the event, make sure you (or a colleague) have a company credit card or that payment can be made on your personal credit card and claimed back.

You'll be surprised how many unexpected expenses pop up on the day. For example, the contract for one event I organised quite clearly stated that the overnight delegate rate included dinner, but neglected to point out that it only consisted of two courses and not the standard three. After a short and somewhat heated argument with the maître d', we came to an arrangement whereby delegates could still have three courses with the additional costs being paid by credit card once dinner was over. There are times when it's wise not to spend your entire budget at once.

Most of the financial aspects have now been worked out. You know who's going to pay for what and who's responsible for authorising payments. You also have an overview of your organisation's financial processes and the name of a contact in the Accounts Department.

The final planning stage task is to take Disraeli's approach and prepare for the worst, yet hope for the best. It's time to draw up a Plan B.

Keeping track checklist

Time to complete: 30-60 minutes.

Aim: To understand the financial processes in your organisation. Don't worry if you don't have all the information to hand at this stage.

Monitoring the budget
- Who is responsible for monitoring the budget?

Negotiating and signing contracts
- Who is responsible for negotiating and/or signing supplier contracts?

Financial processes: speakers
- What are the processes for handling the financial relationship with speakers?
- Is a purchase order required and who is responsible for authorising it?
- How should speakers claim payment?
- How are speakers expected to book accommodation and travel, and is a purchase order required?
- How should speakers claim payment for expenses?

Financial processes: assistants
- What are the processes for handling staff expenses?
- How are members of staff expected to book accommodation and travel, and is a purchase order required?
- How should staff claim payment for expenses?

Financial processes: services
- What are the financial processes for handling suppliers?
- Is a purchase order required, and who is responsible for authorising it?
- How should suppliers claim payment for their services?

Financial processes: delegates
- If paying delegates' travel or accommodation expenses, what are the processes for handling them?
- How are delegates expected to book accommodation and travel, and is a purchase order required?
- How should delegates claim payment for expenses?

Financial processes: payment methods
- What is the method of payment for speakers, assistants, suppliers, and delegates?

Financial processes: contact
- Who can you contact in case of any queries?

Credit cards
- Do you (as organiser) or any of your colleagues attending the event have a company credit card?
- If not, can you use your personal credit card and claim back any additional expenses?

Chapter 10

PLAN B

Everybody gets sick from time to time or has to deal with a personal emergency, so as the Scout Motto says, "Be prepared." Therefore, should the unexpected happen, all event organisers should have at least one Plan B up their sleeve.

Emergency sessions

Unfortunately, by the law of averages, the following situation is bound to happen at least once: after meticulously planning everything, one of the speakers notifies you on the morning of the event that she can no longer attend. Suddenly, there is an empty session in the agenda with only minutes to spare before the keynote begins. You now have two options: panic like crazy or smile serenely because you have already prepared for this eventuality.

Most of the suggested emergency sessions below do not require much preparation prior to the event. Simply decide which approach will be most suitable depending on the size of gap in the agenda and the event type. You can use one or a combination of the following:

- extend sessions
- hold a discussion session
- convene a panel session
- run an open mike (show and tell) session
- give a pre-prepared presentation

Extend sessions

This is a useful emergency strategy should a speaker pull out at the last minute. Simply extend each session and/or break by five minutes or so. In any case, agenda items that involve a discussion, question and answer section, or workshop often overrun. For example, adding an extra five minutes to four sessions will fill up the void left by a twenty minute presentation.

Try to spread any sudden gap in the agenda across the schedule as a whole because it will be less noticeable. People are there to get as much as they can from the event and an extra five minutes of discussion or question and answer can be valuable.

Realistically, this can only be done once during an event and the session in question must be fairly short (less than thirty minutes). If more than one agenda item is affected or the session is much longer, combine this approach with one or more of the other options.

Discussion session

Depending on the number of people attending, split the audience into groups and ask them to discuss a particular topic amongst themselves. Ask for a representative from each group to feed back over the course of a couple of minutes to the rest of the audience. If there are fewer than thirty people in the session, the discussion can take place within the group as a whole with someone (probably you as organiser) acting as facilitator.

Ideally, this should be prepared in advance, but it is possible to think on your feet and base the discussion on issues that crop up during the event.

Panel session

Ask all the speakers to sit at the front and take questions from the audience either on a topic prepared in advance or based on issues that have arisen so far. This can be a useful approach to thrashing out solutions and gives delegates the opportunity to access a panel of experts.

Open mike (show and tell)

In this session, members of the audience volunteer to spend five minutes or so talking about a relevant topic close to their heart. This requires a facilitator to ensure that speakers stick to their allotted time.

Volunteers may not always be forthcoming, at least not initially. One approach is to spend five minutes at the beginning of the session asking delegates to write down a topic they would like to talk about (not everyone will want to do this, which is fine). Gather up the submissions and pull out each one at random. If people are still reluctant to come forward, you may have step up to the mike yourself for five minutes. This often encourages people and once the ball starts rolling, it can be hard to stop.

Pre-prepared session

This requires some preparation in advance. Prepare an item, such as a presentation or practical session that could be used to fill an unexpected gap. Consider using a presentation from a previous event if the audience is unlikely to have heard it before.

Emergency staffing

It is not only speakers who may be affected by illness and personal emergencies. This can also happen to the organiser as well as staff assisting at the event. Therefore, you will need to draw up one Plan B to cover absence of the organiser/meeting facilitator (that is probably you), and one to cover absence of assistants.

Organiser absence

As sole organiser and meeting facilitator with no colleagues to assist, my worst fear was not being able to attend on the day due to illness or personal emergency. It can happen, which is why it is important to have a Plan B in place. If other members of staff are helping to run the event, at least the baton can be passed on to them.

Always prime your company (or colleagues assisting you) to prepare for such an eventuality, which whilst very rare, can occasionally happen. Draw up a battle plan just in case and ensure that your organisation can send someone to replace you.

Put together a bare-bones pack that can be left on your desk or online in a staff repository or other file hosting service. You only need enough information for someone to be able to run the event in your stead, rather than a huge amount of detail. Ensure that the following is included:

- **venue details:** venue name, address, contact name, and telephone number, details of any overnight accommodation or other special requirements
- **meeting details:** agenda, master delegate list, location of badges (optional as an event will still run smoothly without them), location of workshop materials, links to presentations and other virtual information, Plan B: Emergency session (essential if you were also scheduled to give a presentation)
- **other relevant information**

Your replacement should notify the venue of the situation so that delegates can be kept informed, especially if he or she is likely to be late arriving at the event.

Staff absence

Should an assistant be unable to attend on the day, this additional Plan B is particularly important if parallel sessions are scheduled because it's difficult to be in two places at the same time. Depending on the nature of the parallel session, either ask one of the speakers to facilitate it or replace it with a Plan B: Emergency session.

If you're fortunate enough to have more than one colleague assisting you, the role can be divided amongst the other assistants. In any case, it's often possible to do everything yourself on the day even if it does require superhuman effort.

Hopefully, you'll never need to use your Plan Bs. However, it does take a huge weight off your shoulders knowing that you are prepared for the worst.

It may have taken a little while, but the planning stage is now complete. You know the event's aims and objectives and how many people to invite (design brief). You have a draft agenda and have thought about speakers for each session. You also have a venue brief and have even worked out a rough date. Finally, you have researched the financial aspects and developed a set of Plan Bs in case of emergency.

Now we're going to move things up a gear and start organising the event.

Plan B checklist

Time to complete: 30-60 minutes.

Aim: To draw up your Plan Bs.

Plan B 1: emergency sessions
- Consider the options and prepare your Plan B.

Plan B 2: organiser absence
- Draw up a Plan B in case you, as facilitator, cannot attend on the day. Who will replace you?
- Where will you leave your bare-bones pack?

Plan B 3: staff absence
- Draw up a Plan B in case an assistant is unable to attend. Who will take over their role?

STAGE 2: ORGANISING

Chapter 11

JUGGLING SKILLS REQUIRED

After laying the foundations (planning), the next stage is to focus on the logistical aspects of the event (organising).

There are three inter-related components that must come together at the same time: date, speakers, and venue. Unless fortune is smiling, it can take a bit of juggling to get everything to fall into place. For example, your favourite venue may be available on the right date, however your must-have speaker is out of the country that day. Or amazingly, all the speakers are available and keen to take part in the event, but every venue in your chosen location is booked solid for the next six months.

This part of the process never runs smoothly. Until these three components are in place, it's almost impossible to move forward. A good strategy is to start with any one of the three elements and try to fit the rest in place around it. Choose the strongest candidate to set the pace. For example, if the choice of date is crucial, establish that first. If the venue is important, start with its available dates. If you must have a particular speaker, set the event date according to his/her availability.

From now on everything is time-oriented, so the checklists for the organising stage will appear at the end of the section rather than at the end of each chapter.

Chapter 12

INVITING SPEAKERS

As we have to start somewhere, this chapter takes the plunge by focussing on speaker availability as the strongest component. However, you could begin by booking the venue or establishing a date.

Invitations

From the list of potential speakers you drew up during the planning stage, you now need to ascertain their availability and whether they are interested in being involved.

If it is vital that a particular speaker take part in the event and timescales are flexible, ask them to provide you with their availability on a preselected range of dates (essentially you're asking the speaker to set the date for you). Once these two elements are in place, it is simply a case of securing the rest of the speakers and the venue.

When contacting potential speakers, include the following details in the invitation:

- **event aims:** title, purpose, benefits
- **audience:** type of audience, likely audience numbers
- **location:** rough (or set) geographical location
- **date:** rough (or set) date
- **session:** subject matter, type, and length of session required

- **fees:** whether expenses will be paid; request details of the speaker's fees
- **deadline:** for responding to the invitation

You should already have all this information at your fingertips from the design brief, draft agenda, and venue brief.

At this stage, it doesn't matter if the meeting title is still provisional. If the event aims are clear, a potential speaker can decide whether they are able to contribute. By providing information about the type and size of audience, a presenter can then tailor their session accordingly. If the exact geographical area still hasn't been decided, provide a general location or part of the country where the event is likely to be held.

Start the ball rolling by providing some rough dates and asking the speaker whether or not they are free at that time. Online scheduling tools, such as **Meet-O-Matic**[2], can be particularly helpful when co-ordinating the availability of more than one person.

When drawing up the invitation, the most important aspect is outlining what is expected from the speaker. Provide them with an idea of the topic area, type, and length of session. Depending on the number of accepted invitations, you may need to increase or decrease the length of each session.

In other words, it is always worth sending out more invitations than necessary in case some people aren't available. Play around with the timings of the agenda by adding or subtracting five to ten minutes from each session depending on the number of available speakers. Presenters can be then be asked to prepare a slightly shorter or longer session, but do this as soon as you can.

If a speaker charges a fee that is beyond the reach of the budget, try to negotiate a better rate or if appropriate, offer something mutually beneficial in return, such as an opportunity to work with your company as a consultant. Some presenters may reduce or waive their fees if they are speaking to educational or non-profit organisations.

Provide a time limit for potential speakers to respond to the invitation. This is especially important if you're working to a deadline. Allow seven working days for a response and if there is no answer, give them a gentle

---

[2] http://www.meetomatic.com/calendar.php

nudge and ask for a reply within another five days or so. However, don't hassle them. If there is still no answer, move on, and look for someone else.

Keep a list of invited speakers and their response. Add any additional information, such as title and brief description of session, equipment and/or accommodation requirements, and bio (biography). This will make it easier when the time comes to flesh out the agenda.

> **Tip:** If it is proving impossible to find that final speaker, consider running a Plan B Emergency session.

Confirming speakers

As soon as the initial invitation is accepted, ensure the speaker is definitely booked for the event by confirming the following information with them:

- the actual **date** and double-check their availability
- the actual **location** (if you have it)
- **payments** (such as fees, travel expenses, or accommodation) and how to claim them (expenses form or invoice)
- **session** type, length, and subject area
- whether the session is for everyone or just a subset of the **audience** (for example, a parallel strand or session)
- how to **register**: provide a link to the event registration site or state that you will do it for them

You will also need to ask them to provide:

- a **title and brief description** of their session to go on the agenda and event website
- a short **bio** (optional)
- **requirements** for materials in terms of technology or workshop items, for example

79

- their **presentation** on a USB pen drive or online file hosting service, such as **Dropbox**[3], for preloading onto a laptop or event USB pen drive, and for adding to the bare-bones pack
- **accommodation requirements** (optional)

Remember to set a deadline for a response. Start with seven working days and gently prompt people thereafter.

Finalising the agenda

Once speakers have replied to the confirmation, flesh out the agenda with the session title, name of speaker, and a brief description of session.

Increase or decrease session and break lengths, or move agenda items around so that the event flows seamlessly from one topic to another.

Once invitations have been sent out and any must-have speakers confirmed, the venue can then be booked (or, as mentioned earlier, secure the venue first if that is more important).

---

[3] http://www.dropbox.com/

Chapter 13

BOOKING THE VENUE

Unless you already have somewhere in mind, it can take a little while to research and find a suitable venue. Therefore, the information captured in the draft agenda and venue brief will make life easier when describing your event's requirements.

Once you have selected a venue, there are a number of aspects you may need to discuss including:

- delegate rates
- additional requirements, such as accommodation, and technology
- catering options
- accessibility
- contract and cancellation policies

As mentioned at the beginning of this stage, your key priority is either the date or the venue. In other words, if the date is important, you can choose anywhere that has vacancies at that time; but if the venue itself is key, you are limited to its available dates.

Finding a venue

When you drew up the design brief during the planning stage, one of the requirements was the selection of a geographical location. The next step is to pinpoint a city or town in that area that is relatively easy to access and which has a suitable venue available.

When looking for somewhere to hold the event, start with the easy options and then work through to the harder ones. For example, book a venue that is already known or recommended. If it is not available or is unsuitable for your event, ask the venue staff to suggest an alternative or start searching online.

When looking on the internet, try the search term "conference venues [name of town or city]". Once a suitable candidate has been found, check out hotel and venue review sites to get an overall feel of customer satisfaction.

Try to find somewhere that is around ten minutes' walk (urban areas) or public transport/taxi ride (rural or suburban locations) from the nearest major transport hub. Work out how far away the venue is from this hub so that people don't have to take too many different modes of transport.

If most delegates are expected to fly in, aim for a location that is around thirty minutes by taxi or public transport from the airport. If most people are likely to drive, find a venue that is around ten to fifteen minutes from the nearest motorway junction.

If time or staff resources are short, conference booking agents can find and secure a venue for a fee. However, be aware that the contract is with the agent and not with the actual venue. This can add an extra level of communication resulting in a series of email exchanges or telephone calls. For example, if a change needs to be made to any part of the booking, you first have to contact the agent, who contacts the venue, who gets back to the agent, who finally gets back to you.

Tip: It is not always necessary to visit a conference site prior to booking as long as you do your research and exercise your judgement. Visit the venue's website to try and get a feel for the place and to ascertain the room layouts. Look at any available photos, do an image search on the internet, and check out review websites.

Delegate rates

Once a potential venue has been identified, look for the delegate rates on its website. To decide whether you can afford to hold the event there, simply multiply that rate by the expected number of attendees. Sometimes a venue will run a special offer, especially during quieter times of the year. Prices for extras, such as breakout rooms, equipment hire, and conference dinner aren't always advertised, so contact the conference office for further information.

Day delegate rates usually include:

- hire of main conference room
- refreshments at mid-morning and mid-afternoon
- lunch
- projector and screen hire, and one flip chart (although there may be an additional charge for these items)

If the event is shorter than a day, it is sometimes possible to obtain a reduced rate.

Overnight delegate rates usually include:

- everything in the day delegate rate
- accommodation and breakfast
- conference dinner

There is usually a charge for additional items, such as audio-visual equipment, technical support, breakout rooms, conference dinner, and internet access. However, some venues are more generous than others and may include Wi-Fi, unlimited beverages, or stationery packs as standard.

If the total cost of the delegate rates alone will take you close to your budget's limit, consider negotiating with the venue to try and get any additional items included in the fee. However, it really depends on the venue, your relationship with them, and your requirements. For example, if an additional breakout room is only needed for an hour or so, try coming to an arrangement where it is included as part of the fee.

Sometimes it is possible to mix and match rates. For example, if staff and speakers only are staying over the night before, it is usually possible to agree to an overnight delegate rate for them, and a day delegate rate for the rest of the audience.

If delegates are required to stay at the venue or a nearby hotel and they have to book and pay for their own accommodation, arrange a special bed and breakfast rate for them. Usually, the venue or hotel will issue a booking code that delegates must use in order to get a preferential rate. Remember to include this code in your registration confirmation email to delegates.

Accommodation

Some conference locations have hotel facilities, whilst others do not. Depending on the choice of venue, accommodation may have to be found nearby. If so, look for somewhere that is no more than ten minutes' walk away, and remember to include breakfast.

If it is proving difficult to find a venue in your chosen area, look further afield or select a different region.

> **Tip:** If a rural location is preferred or the majority of delegates are likely to have more than a two hour journey to get there, include an overnight stay for all attendees to ensure that they can get to the event on time.

Catering

Always check exactly what refreshments are included in the delegate rate. Beverages usually include tea and coffee. Ideally, non-caffeinated drinks, such as herbal tea and/or water, should also be offered. Most venues now include these options as standard, but some do not.

Ask the venue how they manage refreshment breaks and the conference dinner (if booking one). Refreshments may be served in the main conference room, in a separate room, in a public area, or in the venue's restaurant. There may not be much choice regarding where they are served, but if the location is important, then discuss your requirements with the conference office. For example, a working group may have such a packed agenda that it is easier and more efficient for all refreshments to be served in the main conference room. Remember to add the location to the agenda.

If lunch is a sit-down affair, the venue may require dishes to be pre-selected from a menu or you may just have to take pot-luck. Most conference venues in the United Kingdom offer a vegetarian option as standard, although this is not always the case in other parts of the world. However, you should always check, particularly if this is an important requirement for your event.

If pre-selecting from a buffet menu, ensure that around half the dishes are vegetarian so that people who don't eat meat can feast on more than just the garnish. I have attended several events where the vegetarians have been left to pick out the scraps because the meat-eaters had eaten all the vegetarian options. Nowadays, many venues automatically provide both vegetarian and meat dishes for a buffet, which takes out a lot of the guesswork.

Make sure the venue is aware of any special dietary requirements such as vegetarian, gluten-free, dairy-free, halal, kosher, etc. Most venues are generally adept at handling such requests. Information relating to delegates' special dietary requirements should be gathered when people register and the venue should be informed no later than a week before the event.

When booking a conference dinner, always include water, but if the budget will stretch consider offering wine (usually one bottle of red and one of white per table of six) or a non-alcoholic drink. If trying to keep costs down, book a venue with a bar so delegates can purchase their own drinks. Be aware that there is usually an additional charge for bottled water, so either try to get this included in the rate or ask for jugs of tap water (but do check if there is a charge, as it is not always free).

A conference dinner held at the venue will generally be itemised as part of the final invoice or included in the overnight delegate rate. However, if booking an external restaurant, ensure you know how you are going how to pay for it in advance. A credit card should be sufficient for a small number of people (30 or fewer, for example) dining at a modest restaurant, but make sure the credit card limit is sufficient to cover it. Otherwise, negotiate a menu and ask the restaurant to provide an invoice, but be aware that many places are not able to do this.

Technology

Many venues include hire of a projector and screen as part of the delegate rate. However, some do charge extra.

If it is important to keep costs down, take your own projector. However, unless you have access to a spare one or a replacement bulb, hire the venue's projector rather than take your own because if it fails they are responsible for providing an alternative. Otherwise, try to negotiate for projector hire to be included in the delegate rate.

If playing a video or teaming up with colleagues via a video-conference link, then audio speakers, a microphone, and possibly even technical assistance will be necessary. These items usually cost extra.

Some venues include Wi-Fi as part of the delegate rate, whilst others do not. If trying to keep costs down and internet access isn't an essential part of the event, you don't need to have it. However, do tell delegates beforehand so they can make their own arrangements if it is important to them. Lack of Wi-Fi can have benefits because delegates are more likely to pay attention to speakers rather than check their social media accounts or email.

Accessibility

In the United Kingdom, all public buildings should be accessible to people with disabilities, such as wheelchair or assistance dog users. However, if delegates with particular accessibility requirements are attending, check whether there are likely to be any problems accessing specific parts of the venue. For example, building work or lift maintenance can make it impossible for people with mobility problems to access meeting rooms.

Also, assistance dogs need access to water and an area where they can relieve themselves. Some venues are kind enough to provide water and a bowl. Ask the conference office for suggestions regarding toilet arrangements for animals, otherwise as organiser, you'll be asked to provide directions to the nearest patch of grass.

Some conference venues have audio induction loop technology installed in meeting rooms to support people with hearing disabilities.

Procuring the venue

In order to check whether a venue is suitable, it is often quicker to telephone the conference office and discuss the following basic details:

- date
- size of audience
- number of meeting rooms
- special requirements, such as conference dinner or accommodation

You may need to contact several venues in order to get a match with the date and budget. Once a positive answer has been received, go into more detail and negotiate a rate to cover everything outlined in the venue brief, such as:

- date
- expected number of delegates
- start and finish times
- size and number of meeting rooms
- room layout and furniture
- approximate times for refreshments and any special or additional catering requirements
- other items, such as technology, conference dinner, bar, or accommodation

Send the conference office an email outlining the exact requirements so that both parties know what is expected and the appropriate contract can be drawn up by the venue. Always ensure that any agreements are made in writing, even for a provisional booking, otherwise it can be lost at the drop of a hat. Note that the reservation is never secured until the contract is signed, although most venues will hold a provisional booking for a week or so.

Once the final contract has been received, make sure everything is correct, particularly the date. Mistakes do happen and you don't want to discover that the venue has been booked for the wrong day. Items such as additional breakout rooms or refreshments can often be added once the contract has been agreed. However, it is harder to take things away without paying a financial penalty, so make sure the contract meets your requirements before signing.

Cancelling the event

Always read the venue (and other suppliers') cancellation policy before you sign any contracts.

Having to cancel an event once the contract has been signed is an organiser's worst nightmare. However, in twelve years of running one and two-day events on my own, I have only had to cancel one. Should it be necessary to call the whole thing off, do it no later than two days before the meeting is due to start. Contact everyone by email and phone to make sure they don't start travelling, and refund any attendance fees. Depending on the size of the event and the ramifications should cancellation be necessary, it might be sensible to purchase event insurance if your company policy doesn't already cover it.

Once the three key components of date, speakers, and venue have dropped into place, the rest of the organising stage should be straightforward.

Now the next step is to find the audience.

Chapter 14

INVITING DELEGATES

There is no point holding a meeting without an audience. However, before advertising or sending out invitations, ensure that systems are in place to capture delegate details.

Capturing registration details

The first step is to decide how people are going to register for the event. There are several options:

- **manual:** ask people to contact you via phone, email, or letter
- **automatic (internal):** set up an online registration form on your organisation's website
- **automatic (external):** use an online event ticketing service

Whilst it is possible to manually sign up people, unless there are fewer than ten delegates, you're just creating more work for yourself. As you're likely to add the details to a spreadsheet anyway, why not use an automated process?

Asking people to register online will give you access to all the data necessary for generating badges, delegate lists, email lists, and other documentation. If setting up your own registration form on your organisation's website, you will either need some web design experience or access to a computer administrator who can do this for you. However, hardly any technical skills are necessary when using an online event ticketing service, such as **EventBrite**[4].

Before diving straight into designing the registration form (whether online or offline), jot down a list of all the data you need to capture and the order in which it should appear. This will make life easier when the time comes to create the final version. Here are some details that could be collected (an asterisk denotes that it is essential and should be captured for all events):

- first name*
- last name*
- organisation (unless inviting members of the general public)*
- email address*
- telephone number*
- special requirements (dietary and access)*
- accommodation requirements
- attendance at conference dinner
- other information, such as project name
- payment method
- address for invoice

Always test online forms with dummy data before going live. The registration page or associated website should provide details about the event, such as:

- event title*
- date and time*
- location*
- aim
- benefits or highlights
- how to register and the deadline (around 5-7 working days before the actual event)*
- cost for attending and payment method*
- what's included (such as conference dinner or accommodation)*

---

[4] http://www.eventbrite.co.uk/

- accommodation details (if delegates are expected to book their own)
- agenda

Remember to ask speakers and assistants to sign up, as well as yourself (this is also a good opportunity to double-check that the registration process is working as expected). Every single attendee, no matter what their role, should register so that you can provide the venue with exact numbers along with a list of any special requirements. Close registration seven days before the event so there is time to contact the venue with the details they require.

Invitations

Once the event information and registration page has been set up, it can then be advertised. When sending invitations direct to prospective delegates or when advertising the event more widely, remember to include:

- date*
- location*
- cost*
- link to the event website*
- how to register and the deadline (around 5-7 working days before the actual event)*
- aim of the event
- benefits or highlights

All other details, such as travel information, can be displayed on the event's website.

Start to advertise the event approximately six weeks beforehand. Ask all prospective delegates to register, even if the meeting is private and people have been told about it in advance. Send out a reminder three weeks before and a final notice ten days before the actual date.

Waiting lists

Set up a waiting list after registration has closed or if the event proves to be popular. Some delegates will cancel after they have registered because they can no longer attend. If people really want to come to the event and are unable to register, they will often contact the organiser direct. Run the waiting list on a first-come, first-served basis.

Generally, around 5% of delegates do not turn up on the day, so it is possible to squeeze in a few latecomers just before the event. If registration has already closed, ask people to provide their details via email and manually add them to the registration system.

Confirmation

Always send a confirmation email to delegates as soon as they have registered. This can normally be set up as an automated service if using your organisation's website or an online event ticketing service.

If this isn't possible, draw up a confirmation email that can be sent out manually each time somebody registers. Delegates expect to receive confirmation as soon as they sign up, so don't take too long to email people when taking this approach. If several people register at a time, send out a batch of emails at least once a day.

The following information should be included in the confirmation email:

- date*
- start and finish times*
- location and how to get there (usually a link to the venue)*
- confirmation of payment received (if charging delegates to attend)*
- accommodation details
- link to the agenda
- link to the event website*
- if documentation is not being printed, provide an online link
- special instructions, such as whether delegates need to bring anything with them

- ask delegates to contact you if they can no longer attend*
- your contact details*

> **Tip:** It is virtually guaranteed that some people won't read the confirmation email. Therefore, make sure you have this information to hand prior to and during the event.

At this point, the event is almost ready to run. You've arranged the speakers, booked the venue, and invited the audience. The final step is to put together the documentation pack.

Chapter 15

Documentation

It is good ecological and financial practice to keep printing to a minimum. Plus it reduces the weight of your suitcase if you're travelling by public transport to the event.

If delegates with visual impairments are attending, provide an accessible electronic version of any documentation so that it can be accessed via assistive technologies, such as a screen reader (text to speech software) or screen magnifier. Here are a few very basic rules:

- Ensure the text is text and not just an image of it.
- Use heading styles to help navigation.
- PDF (Portable Document Format) files are usually accessible, but some PDF creators lock down documents, which means they cannot be accessed by assistive technologies.
- Use alt (alternative) text to meaningfully describe images.

Further information on web and document accessibility can be found across the internet, but a good starting point is **Making information accessible to all**[5] from the EBU (European Blind Union). In any case, it is good practice to make events as accessible as possible because this usually benefits everyone.

---

[5] http://www.euroblind.org/resources/guidelines/nr/88

Tip: Aim to draw up the documentation as you go along and no later than the week before the event. Then, put together your documentation pack: agenda, delegate lists, badges, signage, and other handouts.

Agenda

As each speaker confirms his or her attendance, update the agenda with the exact timing, speaker name, session title, and description.

Delegates like to know what to expect on the day (especially when it is time to eat!), so make the agenda available online, in paper format, or both. Generally, if the agenda is longer than one double-sided page of A4, email or put it online as a PDF and mention this in the confirmation email. This reduces costs in terms of time, money, and the environment. If it is no more than one double-sided page of A4, print one copy for each delegate or make it available electronically. In this case, provide a condensed one-page version so people have an overview of the structure of the event.

Unless you're using an external printing service, print off the agenda as close to the start of the event as possible as there will always be one or two last minute changes. Two days beforehand is usually sufficient to give you some leeway in case of printer malfunction.

Tip: Regardless of the agenda length, print off a few copies for yourself and any assistants, plus one or two spare copies. A hard copy will be invaluable for scribbling down any sudden changes to the schedule.

Master delegate list

The master delegate list contains all the details from the registration form, whether online or offline. Sort the information by last name in alphabetical order for ease of reference. Keep it safe because it contains people's contact details and personal information. Use it to:

- Produce anything that requires a delegate's name, such as badges.
- Act as a list of contact details in case of cancellation.
- Check off delegates as they arrive.
- Account for people in case of emergency evacuation.
- Advise the venue of any special requirements.
- Produce a mailing list for follow-up and notification of future events.

If using an online event ticketing service, it should be possible to download everything as a CSV (Comma-Separated Values) file for importing into a spreadsheet or word processing package. The data can then be formatted for ease of use.

Create an edited version of the list to take with you containing key information, such as:

- first name
- last name
- organisation
- email address
- telephone number
- special requirements (dietary and access)
- other information, such as accommodation requirements

To keep as much of the information together as possible, set the print area so that all the columns can be printed on one page. If there are a large number of delegates, the rows will print over several pages. Occasionally, people will send a colleague if they are unable to attend, so leave some space to handwrite any changes on the day.

Take a couple of copies of the master delegate list with you so that delegates can be checked off as they arrive. It is often useful to have a spare.

Delegate list (for delegates)

This delegate list is a subset of the information from the master delegate list and is given out in the event documentation pack. It usually includes:

- first name
- last name
- organisation
- email address

Providing a delegate list can help people network and collaborate, and can act as a simple reminder for any follow-up action after the event. As it is easy to harvest email addresses from an electronic delegate list, give out a paper copy to make it harder for people to send spam emails. Such practices are frowned upon and there is generally an element of trust, but it can still happen.

Format the delegate list for ease of use. Print off one for each attendee, plus a couple of spare ones, just in case.

Badges

Badges: the curate's egg of meetings. The good part is that they are helpful for people who don't know each other and by the second day of an event, most people have taken them off anyway. However, be aware that some venues require delegates to wear badges at all times for security reasons. If this is the case, mention it in the housekeeping speech.

The bad part is that they are the bane of an event organiser's life. This is the best time for the printer to chew up the only inserts you have; to suddenly discover that a colleague has borrowed all the badge holders; for the computer to die; and for last minute delegates to pop out of the woodwork.

Therefore, order in advance plenty of badge inserts and badge holders that actually fit together, and keep them stashed away from colleagues. Otherwise, you may end up cobbling together badges from leftovers and cutting down large inserts to fill small holders.

Use the master delegate list and your word processing software's mail merge function to create the badges. Follow its instructions from beginning to end and always do a practice run first. It is amazing how easy it is to mess this up. Badges only need to show the first name, last name, and organisation. Use the largest font possible for the label/insert size and make sure each field fits neatly on one line. Sometimes a bit of manual formatting is necessary to accommodate particularly long words.

To avoid waste and reduce costs, ask delegates to return their badges at the end of the event. Some venues require people to sign in and wear visitor passes in addition to name badges. Remind attendees to return them all during the housekeeping and closing speeches.

Signage

Signage may consist of standalone signs directing delegates to the main conference room, or may simply be a piece of paper displaying the company or event name stuck on the meeting room door. Some venues put up signage as part of the service and will ask you to provide the wording.

If they do not offer to do this or if additional breakout rooms have been booked, print off your own signs. A sheet of A4 in landscape mode, with your organisation's name and the name of the event or session in as large a font as will fit, is usually sufficient. Leave space for any hand-drawn direction arrows or comments, which can be added on the day.

Pack a large marker pen and some blu tack (poster putty) for attaching signs to a door or other surface. This makes it easier for delegates to find the meeting rooms, particularly if they are scattered across the venue.

Other handouts

Keep handouts to a minimum by providing electronic versions where possible. If speakers are happy for their presentations to be put online after the event, there is not much point in distributing hard copies.

Some speakers may ask you to print out documentation for a workshop or practical session, whilst others may bring it with them. Remember to print out anything that may be useful for your Plan B session(s).

Prepare the event pack

There is no point leaving everything until the last minute and getting stressed. If you have followed the *Prepare to Meet* process, there should be plenty of time to put everything together into an event pack. Here is a list of some of the items you'll need to include:

Documentation pack
- **Agenda:** copies for yourself and assistants, and one for each delegate (if taking this approach), plus a couple of spares.
- **Master delegate list:** two to three copies.
- **Delegate list (for delegates):** one for each attendee, plus a couple of spares.
- **Badges:** pre-prepared, plus a couple of blank inserts and holders.
- **Signage:** five should be ample.
- **Other handouts:** include anything necessary for your Plan B session(s).

Stationery pack
- Blu tak (poster putty).
- Fine-tipped marker pens for writing badges.
- A few sheets of paper for booking taxis or taking impromptu notes.
- White board or other thick markers for flip charts and signage.
- A pack of sticky notes (useful for Plan B sessions).

Technology
- Laptop.
- Other technology.
- Mobile (cell) phone.
- If using an Apple Mac, take a Mini DisplayPort to DVI (or VGA or HDMI) adaptor for attaching the laptop to a projector. Some older projectors are only able to connect to Windows laptops, but check with the venue first as they may have an adaptor.

Personal information
- Contact details for the venue.
- Copy of the contract(s) with the venue and other suppliers.
- Map of how to reach the venue.
- Public transport timetables.
- Overnight accommodation details.

Put the pack together a few days before the event and double-check it before you set off.

The following checklist and timetable assumes you have at least six weeks in which to plan and organise the event. Of course, it is always possible to speed up or slow down the process.

Chapter 16

ORGANISING STAGE CHECKLIST

This checklist is also a timetable that itemises what you need to do and when during the organising stage. Depending on your event's requirements, not every item will be of relevance. There may also be delays as people take time to respond to emails. However, things will eventually fall into place.

Week 1 (6 weeks before the event)

Agenda
- Add session titles and descriptions to the agenda as you receive them.
- Prepare your Plan B sessions.

Documentation
- Order badge holders and inserts.
- Order other stationery and materials.

Invitations
- Set up the event website, registration page, and confirmation email (or use an online ticketing service).
- Put a refund mechanism in place should the event be cancelled.

Speakers

- Invite speakers.
- Send a confirmation email to speakers who accept the invitation.
- Add speaker bios (biographies) to the event website as you receive them.
- Keep a list of invited speakers, their response, session details, equipment requirements, accommodation requirements, etc.

Venue

- Research venues.
- Negotiate a day or overnight delegate rate.
- Make menu selections.
- Ask the venue how/where refreshments/conference dinner will be served.
- Check the venue is accessible if delegates with disabilities are expected.
- Check whether signage is included.
- Check the venue's badge policy.
- If taking a laptop, check whether the venue will supply an adaptor for the projector (or purchase your own).
- Book the venue plus any additional requirements, such as technology, conference dinner, accommodation, bar, entertainment, etc.
- If using facilities outside of the venue, research and book an external restaurant for the conference dinner, a suitable pub/bar, entertainment, accommodation, etc.
- Receive contracts from the venue and other supplier(s), check the cancellation policies, check all details, sign and return.
- Consider insuring the event in case of cancellation.
- Book accommodation for assistants or speakers.

Week 2

Agenda
- Add session titles and descriptions to the agenda as you receive them.

Invitations
- Send out email invitations to prospective delegates (except speakers).
- Advertise the event.
- Send out manual confirmation emails (if not using automated email confirmations).

Speakers
- Gently nudge speakers who haven't responded to the original invitation (give them another five days).
- Contact other potential speakers if the first batch of speakers cannot attend.
- Send a confirmation email to speakers who accept the invitation during this week.
- Add speaker bios to the event website as you receive them.
- Update the list of invited speakers, their response, session details, equipment requirements, accommodation requirements, etc.
- Check speakers have registered to attend the event and nudge those who have not.

Venue
- Book any additional assistant or speaker accommodation.

Week 3

Agenda
- Add session titles and descriptions to the agenda as you receive them.
- Finalise the agenda and tweak timings if necessary.

Invitations
- Send out manual confirmation emails (if not using automated email confirmations).

Speakers
- Ignore speakers who still haven't responded.
- Send a confirmation email to speakers who accept an invitation during this week.
- Add speaker bios to the event website as you receive them.
- Update the list of invited speakers, their response, session details, equipment requirements, accommodation requirements, etc.
- Check speakers have registered to attend the event and nudge those who have not.

Venue
- Book any additional assistant or speaker accommodation.

Week 4

Invitations
- Send out a reminder email to prospective delegates.
- Contact speakers who haven't yet registered.
- Re-advertise the event.

- Send out manual confirmation emails (if not using automated email confirmations).

Week 5

Documentation
- Design and print signage.

Invitations
- Send out a final call to prospective delegates.
- Contact speakers who haven't yet registered.
- Close registration 5 days before the event.
- Set up a waiting list and contact people as soon as possible should someone drop out.
- Send out manual confirmation emails (if not using automated email confirmations).

Venue
- Provide the venue with the exact number of delegates, along with any special dietary and access requirements.
- Provide external caterers (or restaurant) for conference dinner with the exact number of delegates, along with any dietary and access requirements.
- Provide the venue or external supplier with exact numbers for entertainment and any special access requirements.
- Provide the venue or external hotel with exact numbers for accommodation, along with any special access or room requirements.

You
- Get plenty of early nights and schedule time for relaxation.

Week 6 (the week of the event)

Agenda
- Load speaker presentations onto a USB pen drive or file sharing service, and preload onto your laptop.
- Update the event website and agenda with any changes.

Cancelling the event
- Contact everyone by email and phone no later than two days before the event is due to start.

Documentation
- Print off any documentation.
- Prepare badges.
- Prepare the event pack.
- Prepare the bare-bones pack.

Invitations
- Contact people on the waiting list as soon as someone drops out and manually register them.
- Send out manual confirmation emails (if not using automated email confirmations).

You
- Get plenty of early nights and schedule time for relaxation. You're going to need it!

Now that everything has been planned and organised, it's time to run the event. Good luck!

Stage 3: On The Day

Chapter 17

FIRST CHECKS

The big day has arrived. All the preparation is over and you're ready to take the stage.

Arrive at the venue at least one hour before the Registration session because you need to check that everything has been arranged as outlined in the contract (you should have a copy in your event pack). In any case, there are always one or two delegates who arrive early and you should be there to greet them.

Now is the time to rectify any mistakes or booking errors, confirm the housekeeping arrangements, and check that meeting rooms have been furnished correctly.

There is a checklist at the end of this section to help you get through the day.

Housekeeping

Introduce yourself to the conference office or venue contact as soon as you arrive. This gives you the opportunity to find out about the housekeeping arrangements so that you can pass them on to delegates during the Welcome session. Items to check with the venue include:

- **Accessibility:** If assistance dogs are expected, ask the venue to provide something for them to drink from and find out where they can go to relieve themselves. Check whether there are likely to be any problems accessing meeting rooms.

- **Badges:** Check whether people need to sign in/out of the building or wear visitor passes and/or event badges at all times. Establish the arrangements for returning visitor passes.
- **Catering:** Double-check that the catering has been organised as requested, find the physical location where refreshments will be served (if not in the meeting rooms), and find out who to contact in case of any problems.
- **Emergency drills:** Ask whether fire alarm tests or other emergency drills are expected. Locate the nearest fire exits, assembly points, toilets, lifts, and staircases for each meeting room.
- **Known issues:** Ask whether there are any maintenance problems that may have an impact on the event, such as building work, technology failure, etc.
- **Signage:** Check the signage provided by the venue or put up your own (ask permission first). To avoid leaving marks, attach signs to wood, plastic, or metal rather than painted walls or fabric. Remember to collect your own signs after the event.
- **Technology:** Ask for the Wi-Fi access details and display them on a flip chart or PowerPoint slide. Check all the technology, such as audio-visual or other equipment, works as expected and find out who to contact in case of a problem.

Accommodation

If your organisation is paying for delegates to stay overnight at the venue, double-check that the correct number and type of rooms have been booked. Make sure that any special arrangements have been honoured, such as booking double or accessible rooms.

Let the venue know if fewer rooms than booked are required. There will always be one or two people who are unable to attend at the last minute and, whilst it may not be possible to recoup the cost, the venue may be able to resell the rooms.

Room layout

Once the peripheral arrangements have been checked, make sure the room layout is correct, and that flip charts or other stationery have been provided.

Don't be afraid to rearrange the furniture, but do ask venue staff to help if moving more than just a couple of chairs. Make sure the registration desk is where you want it to be or ask venue staff to reposition it if necessary.

Lay out badges and documentation packs on the registration table and place workshop or other materials in the meeting room(s).

Set up camp

As soon as all the checks are done, set up camp by choosing the best seat in the house. This is not being selfish. As event organiser, you need to be aware of everything at all times.

Ideally, you should sit at the front, at the end of a row, near the door. Stake your claim before anyone else arrives. If you're introducing speakers, you need to be as close to the front as possible so that you can move around without disturbing other delegates.

By being close to the door, you can quietly sneak out to speak to venue staff and deal with issues that may arise. You can also pop out to check when refreshments are ready. Ensure that any assistants also follow this advice.

If running the event on your own with no-one to help, put badges and delegate packs on the table inside the main conference room in case you're busy elsewhere. It is also a good way to get to know delegates and put faces to names. When you have a spare moment, review which badges have been taken and check off delegates from the master delegate list.

Just before your guests turn up, grab a cup of coffee, and take five minutes to breathe and relax. Make the most of it, as this will probably be the only time you get to yourself for the rest of the day.

Chapter 18

LOOKING AFTER GUESTS

As organiser (either alone or with assistants), you will be on-call throughout the whole day. Your role will fluctuate between champion listener and fount of information, interspersed with periods of troubleshooting, networking, and cajoling. You will also be called upon to present, facilitate, arbitrate, and summarise. In short, you won't have a moment to yourself, but as meetings are about bringing people together, it's definitely worth it!

Registration

Wherever the registration table is located, arrange the badges in the same order as the master delegate list (in alphabetical order by surname). Lay out any documentation, such as the agenda or document pack, alongside.

Check off delegates as they take their badges or alternatively, a few minutes before the event is due to start, highlight everyone who has not yet shown up so you know exactly who is in the room.

As speakers sign in, have a quick chat with them to ensure that they have everything they need and that they know what to do and when.

There will be some absentees on the day, as well as one or two unregistered delegates, who thought they would come along anyway. Usually, the two balance each other out, so it shouldn't be a problem. However, tell the venue as soon as possible if you end up with more delegates than expected, especially if lunch is a sit-down affair or a conference dinner has been booked, because the venue will cater for exact rather than approximate numbers.

Sometimes delegates bring spouses, colleagues, or children. As you have included spare badges in your event pack, this shouldn't be a problem. Add their details to the master delegate list and make them feel especially welcome because they will probably feel like interlopers. Try to make a point of chatting with unexpected delegates at least once during the event. A warm welcome will help people feel more engaged, even if it is not their subject area.

On one occasion, a speaker brought his ten-year old daughter because his childcare arrangements had fallen through. Most children are generally well-behaved at events like this and she had brought some books to read. After her father had finished speaking, I asked her at the coffee break what she thought of his twenty-minute presentation. She said she thought he talked too much!

It does relieve some of the pressure if an assistant is available to welcome and register people, but you can also do it on your own if necessary. Make sure your assistant staffs the registration desk until approximately thirty minutes after the event starts. Badges and document packs can then be brought into the main conference room and any latecomers registered as they arrive.

If you're alone and have to manage registration as well as run the Welcome session, move everything to a table just inside the door of the main conference room and keep an eye out for latecomers. If transport is delayed and dozens of delegates arrive after the event has started, ask them to pick up their badges at the next suitable occasion (such as at mid-morning break or just before a discussion/workshop session). Otherwise, quietly check them in just before or after the Keynote or succeeding session. Keep track of delegates in case of emergency evacuation of the building.

Taxi list

If the venue is a taxi-ride away from the main public transport hubs, ask the venue to arrange taxis for delegates. However, rather than book 150 taxis all heading for the same station, set up a taxi list. Leave a sheet of paper on the registration desk and ask people to write their name, destination, and time the taxi is required by lunchtime. Take it to the venue coordinator and ask him or her to book taxis according to the list.

Announce this proposal during the Welcome session and then, at the beginning of the afternoon sessions, let people know that taxis have been booked. If anyone has forgotten to put their name on the list, ask them to organise their taxi direct with the venue. Unless there is an agreement with the venue, delegates should pay their own taxi fares.

Facilitating

If you're facilitating the event (such as starting and finishing it, introducing the sessions and speakers), create a positive, welcoming mood, and be passionate about the event so that people feel encouraged to engage and interact.

During the Welcome session, pass on any housekeeping information such as:

- Whether a fire alarm test is scheduled.
- Where to assemble in case of emergency evacuation.
- Location of the nearest toilets, lifts, stairs, and emergency exits.
- Where refreshments will be served.
- Arrangements for returning badges and visitor passes.
- Wi-Fi details.
- Any other notices or reminders.

Include a very brief overview of the event, including expected finish and break times, and location of parallel sessions.

The responsibility of the facilitator is to introduce each speaker, and to lead any appreciation (such as applause) at the end. You should also ensure that speakers keep to time, so make sure you can see a clock or have some other way of keeping track. Some Q&A (Question and Answer) or discussion sessions can get heated as people engage with the subject, but don't be afraid to interrupt. Allow discussions to overrun by a minute or so, but keep to the agenda timing as much as possible.

When handling Q&A sessions, ask delegates to put their hands up if they have a question and keep a mental note of who is first, then bring each person into the discussion at the appropriate moment. Try to involve everyone. Some people like the sound of their own voice and will take every opportunity to hijack the conversation. Don't be afraid to politely ignore them by giving someone else a chance to speak.

Try to maintain respect in the room. For example, during one Q&A session, two academics with very different views on the subject in question got into a heated debate. The scholarly discussion almost turned into an altercation with fists flying. If people hold the floor for too long or tempers start to flare, don't be afraid to interrupt and divert the argument. Remember that as facilitator, you are in charge and your word is final.

Taking notes

Notes can be used to provide a summary of the meeting for reporting purposes, a list of actions to be taken by the organisers or audience, or feedback on a new product or service. They may be supplied as text, audio (provide a transcript for accessibility), or video (with transcript or captions).

Depending on the purpose and depth of the notes, ask speakers if they are happy for them to be made public. If sessions are being recorded, ask people's permission first. Similarly if videos or photos are made available online, you may need to get written permission from everyone who appears.

When taking notes, be discreet in what you report. Avoid describing anything that may have a negative effect on the speaker or the event.

Refreshments

Make sure you know which delegates have special access or dietary requirements.

If lunch is served as a buffet, a venue will often prepare an individual plate for people with special dietary requirements (such as gluten-free or halal). It may (or may not) be labelled. As people queue up for lunch, locate these individual plates and tell the relevant delegates where to find them.

Should any delegates with disabilities not have a companion, ask if they need help. Depending on their disability and the way in which refreshments are being served, you may need to help them select food or beverages.

If a delegate has an assistance dog, ensure it has access to fresh water and somewhere to relieve itself at break times. You or a colleague may have to accompany them.

If a minimum amount of food for people with special dietary requirements (such as vegetarian, kosher, or halal) has been ordered at a buffet-style meal, make sure those delegates go first in the queue so they don't have to resort to picking out suitable items from the remnants.

> **Tip:** If you have a booked a conference dinner, arrive at least 10-15 minutes beforehand to check that everything has been arranged as requested, including special dietary requirements, water, wine, etc.

Networking

You will have a lot to do, so be strict about carving out time and deal only with the business of the day. Save additional business meetings for a time when you can focus on the matter in hand, unless they will take less than five minutes.

Chat to different people each break time, but don't allow yourself to be captured by one delegate for too long, especially if there are other things you need to do. Be assertive and don't be afraid to move on to talk to someone else.

Find some time for yourself during each recess, even if only for a couple of minutes. Grab a coffee, find a quiet space (the main conference room is usually almost empty at break times), and take five minutes to breathe and re-energise for the next part of the agenda.

Most events do run smoothly, but just in case they don't, the next chapter describes some of the problems you may face.

Chapter 19

TROUBLESHOOTING

As Robert Burns said, "The best-laid schemes o' mice an' men gang aft agley" and even the most perfectly planned meeting can still be at the mercy of outside influences. Unexpected problems can result in people remembering an event for all the wrong reasons, no matter how well it's been organised.

For example, I remember listening to colleagues who had just returned from a three-day conference and all they could talk about was how awful the food was (photos of it filled up the conference's social media streams) and how the keynote speaker swore (albeit mildly). OK, so you can't necessarily control the food or what your speakers say, but it just goes to show how seemingly insignificant details can have a big impact.

Here are some of the things that could happen and suggestions on how to deal with them. Whatever happens, never be afraid to take control of the situation.

Accidents and illness

If someone is taken ill or has an accident, ask your venue contact to get in touch with the designated first aider or call an ambulance yourself. As organiser, you don't need to travel to the hospital with the delegate because your first priority is to run the event. However, contact the hospital as soon as practicable to check on the injured or sick person's health.

At the end of one of my events, a delegate tripped on the kerb and hit his head as he left the venue. The conference centre's designated first aider patched him up, but I took him to the hospital for a check-up and sat with him until he was pronounced fit to go home. I contacted him the next day to check on his health. Fortunately, he was fine.

Depending on the nature and severity of the illness or accident, call an impromptu break or cancel the event. Work with your venue contact to decide on the best course of action.

Delegate delays

Sometimes inclement weather or public transport delays can result in most of the audience arriving considerably late. Unless you know the delay is likely to be less than ten minutes, start the event on time and do a quick recap at a convenient point for latecomers. There will be some disruption as people arrive, but try to keep to the schedule as much as possible.

Fire alarms

Fire alarms have a habit of going off at the wrong time and interrupting the flow of an event. Depending on whether there really is a fire or not, people may have to evacuate the building for twenty minutes or twenty hours.

If the event has only just started and the whole building starts to burn, cancel the event, and send everyone home. What is left of the conference office should reimburse you. If the fire is not serious, but you aren't allowed to return to the venue, and there are only a small number of delegates, consider reconvening at another location, such as a hotel or cafe. You will need to think on your feet and readjust the agenda accordingly.

Always take the master delegate list with you so that a roll call can be taken in case of a real fire or other emergency. Make sure that all your delegates can be accounted for.

If it's simply a false alarm, readjust the agenda by reducing the length of some of the breaks or discussions, or by abandoning a session altogether.

For example, one practical session I attended was being led by a speaker via video link. Unfortunately, the fire alarm went off in the video-conferencing studio and she had to leave. We carried on with the rest of the practical session as best we could and then took an early tea-break. She never did come back!

Speaker no-shows

Sometimes a speaker is unable to attend on the day for whatever reason, be it illness, emergency, or even intimidation from a rival organisation (yes, it can happen, but maybe I was just unlucky). This shouldn't faze you because you have a Plan B. Either readjust the length of the sessions or add your Plan B session to the place where the speaker dropped out.

Remember to adjust the timings on your personal copy of the agenda to keep everyone to the new schedule.

> **Tip:** Rearrange the agenda so that the empty slot is scheduled for as late in the day as possible. This makes it easier to keep track of the extended sessions and allows time for potential discussion topics to arise during the course of the event.

Assistant no-shows

If your sole assistant fails to turn up on the day, you should still be able to do everything on your own, although you will need much more energy.

If the assistant was due to run a session, resort to your preferred Plan B. If he or she were due to facilitate a parallel strand, either ask delegates if they would like to attend a different session or requisition one of the speakers to act as facilitator.

If a delegate you know well is attending, it may be possible to ask them to help with the odd minor task. People are often very willing to assist. For example, a colleague was due to support me at one event, but for whatever reason he didn't turn up. Fortunately, the meeting was hosted by a project partner, who lent me one of their members of staff to assist with registration.

> **Tip:** Thank anyone who has given you a helping hand and write an email or handwritten note of appreciation after the event.

Technology breakdown

Technology breakdown is almost always guaranteed. If this happens to the equipment you have hired the supplier should provide a replacement, but this may take time. Therefore, don't be afraid to adjust the agenda, swap sessions round, or move on to a Q&A (Question and Answer) or discussion session.

If the technology failure happens within five minutes of a scheduled break, send everyone off for tea, but bring them back five minutes earlier to keep the agenda on track. Most technology problems can be sorted out over the course of a tea-break. However, don't spend too long trying to solve the problem; either consider asking delegates if they have any solutions or move on without the technology if possible.

If your laptop fails, ask if someone will be kind enough to lend you theirs (this is why it's useful to have presentations pre-loaded onto a USB stick or online file sharing service). If you've created a welcoming and positive mood, most people will be happy to help.

Hopefully, you won't need to have to deal with such problems, but forewarned is forearmed as they say, and it's always a good idea to be prepared for most, if not all, eventualities.

And now finally, the event is over. You've made it through the day and it's time for everyone to go home. But wait… you're not quite finished yet. There are still one or two bits and pieces to attend to.

Chapter 20

GOING HOME

I know you're tired and it's been a long day, but this won't take long.

Before heading home, ensure the rooms are tidy. Collect any leftover documentation, badges, visitor passes, lost property, etc. Put any stray crockery in one place and remove any of your own signage.

Then, check out with your contact at the conference office and thank the venue staff.

You now have permission to go home and collapse in a heap. I hope all that hard work has paid off and that you and your guests have enjoyed and benefitted from the event.

The checklist that follows will help you get through the event itself.

Just before the whole process can be concluded, there's one more stage to complete. After all that hard work, it's time to write your thank-you notes and discover what improvements can be made for the next event.

Chapter 21

ON THE DAY CHECKLIST

This list takes you through the initial checks that should be made on arrival at the venue. It also offers suggestions regarding how to look after guests and deal with the unexpected. Depending on your event's requirements, not every item will be of relevance.

First checks

- Arrive at least one hour before the Registration session.
- Introduce yourself to the conference office or venue contact.
- **Accessibility:** Ensure there are no access issues. Find out where assistance dogs can relieve themselves. Ask for a water bowl.
- **Accommodation:** Check the correct number and type of bedrooms have been booked and that any special arrangements have been honoured. Tell the venue if fewer rooms are required.
- **Badges:** Confirm the venue's badge policy. Ascertain the arrangements for returning visitor passes.
- **Catering:** Check catering has been organised as requested. Find the location where refreshments will be served. Identify who to contact in case of problems.
- **Emergency drills:** Find out whether fire alarm tests or other emergency drills are anticipated. Locate the nearest assembly points, fire exits, toilets, lifts, and staircases for each meeting room.

- **Known issues:** Ask if building work is taking place or if there are any maintenance problems.
- **Room layout:** Check each room layout is correct, that flip charts and stationery have been provided, and the registration desk is in the correct location. Rearrange furniture if necessary. Lay out badges, documentation packs, and workshop materials.
- **Signage:** Check signage provided by the venue or put up your own (ask permission first).
- **Technology:** Find out how to access the Wi-Fi. Display the details on a flip chart or PowerPoint slide. Check the technology works as expected. Find out who to contact in case of a problem.
- **Set up camp:** Choose the best seat in the house. Stake your claim. Grab a coffee, and take five.

Looking after guests

- **Registration:** Mark off people on the master delegate list. Inform the venue of any additional catering requirements. Check speakers know what they need to do. Identify delegates with special requirements. Bring badges and documentation packs inside the main conference room at the start of the event. Keep an eye out for latecomers.
- **Taxi list:** Ask delegates to add their details to the taxi list by lunchtime. Ask the venue co-ordinator to book taxis. Report this has been done at the beginning of the afternoon sessions.
- **Facilitating:** Create a positive, welcoming mood. Pass on any housekeeping information during the Welcome session. Introduce each speaker and lead the appreciation. Ensure speakers keep to time. Don't be afraid to interrupt. Allow discussions to overrun slightly if necessary, but keep on schedule. Try to involve everyone. Maintain respect in the room.
- **Taking notes:** Check speakers are happy for notes to be made public. If sessions are being recorded, ask for people's permission first. Be discreet.

- **Refreshments:** Locate individual special dietary requirements dishes and guide the relevant delegates toward them first. Assist delegates with disabilities. Check conference dinner arrangements at least 10-15 minutes beforehand.
- **Networking:** Deal only with the business of the day. Chat to different people each break time. Don't be afraid to move on to talk to someone else. Be assertive. Find a couple of minutes to relax and recharge.

Troubleshooting

- **Accidents and illness:** Ask the venue to get in touch with the designated first aider or call an ambulance yourself. Call an impromptu break or cancel the event. Work with the venue contact to decide on the best course of action. Contact the hospital to check on the delegate's health.
- **Delegate delays:** Start the event on time. Do a quick recap at a convenient point for latecomers. Keep to the schedule as much as possible.
- **Fire alarms:** Depending on the situation, cancel the event and send everyone home, relocate, or adjust the agenda. Take the master delegate list with you for a roll call. Ensure you can account for all your delegates.
- **Speaker no-shows:** Go to Plan B (you remembered to prepare it, right?).
- **Assistant no-shows:** For single sessions: go to Plan B. For parallel sessions: ask delegates if they would like to attend a different strand or requisition one of the speakers to facilitate. Thank anyone who has helped.
- **Technology breakdown:** Depending on the situation, adjust the agenda, swap sessions round, move on to a Q&A or discussion session, or take an early break. Ask if delegates can help. If your laptop fails, ask if someone will lend you theirs.

Going home

- Leave the room(s) tidy. Collect leftover documentation, badges, lost property, etc. Put stray crockery in one place. Remove any signage you have put up.
- Check out with your contact at the venue. Thank venue staff.
- Go home and relax.

STAGE 4: AFTER THE EVENT

Chapter 22

Follow-Up

The final stage of the *Prepare to Meet* process is to tie up all the loose ends. One of the first things to do is thank everyone for the part they played in the event, be they speaker, assistant, delegate, or supplier. Without people's interaction and willingness to get together, there would be no expansion of knowledge, no injection of new ideas, and no forward momentum.

As well as showing your appreciation, you also need to find out whether people enjoyed and benefitted from the event. The feedback they give will help you make improvements for the next one.

The checklist and timetable at the end of this chapter itemise the final actions to be taken before the event can be considered complete.

Survey

The easiest way to find out what people thought about the event is to set up an online questionnaire using a survey tool, such as **SurveyMonkey**[6].

Without going into too much detail, the key to designing a good survey is to keep it short. Aim for around five to seven questions that can be answered using check boxes or scales. Always include a text box for additional comments in case people have something they want to say.

---

[6] http://www.surveymonkey.com/

You may already have specific questions to ask delegates, such as whether people found the event useful, and what they did or didn't like about the meeting. If not, go back to the design brief and devise questions that determine whether the event's purpose was met and whether the anticipated benefits were achieved.

Ensure that the survey can be completed anonymously as people are more likely to be honest. However, do include an option for delegates to leave their name and email address, as some people prefer to put their name to their comments.

Include the link to the survey and deadline for completion when sending thank-you emails to everyone. A week or so should be sufficient. Send a reminder about completing the questionnaire a couple of days before closing the survey.

Notes

If posting notes online for delegates to view, decide whose notes to use: yours, those of colleagues or speakers, or an amalgamation. If you have permission from speakers, upload presentations, workshop materials, or other information to your company's website or to a file sharing service, such as **DropBox**[7].

If delegates are expected to complete a set of actions after the event, make any information available privately or if it's not too big, send it via email.

Thank you notes

People like to feel valued, so sending an email or handwritten note of appreciation after the event can help cement relationships. Thank-you notes

---

[7] http://www.dropbox.com/

should be written to the venue (and other suppliers), speakers, delegates, and anyone who helped in an emergency.

To the venue (and other suppliers)

Send an email to your contact at the venue (and other suppliers) thanking them and their staff for their assistance. Highlight anything that was particularly helpful or mention a member of staff who went out of their way to support you. If there were any major issues that could result in a partial refund, be nice; it helps.

To speakers

Send an individualised email highlighting something from their session that was of particular interest and include follow-up information. For example:

- Thank speakers for their presentation/session.
- Check you have permission to make notes or session materials available privately (to delegates) or publicly (anyone).
- Link to online notes and actions required.
- Link to the online survey and include a deadline.
- Link to other information/documentation.
- Announce forthcoming events or other news.
- Remind them to send in their invoice or expenses claim and include a deadline of about two weeks.

To delegates

Send an email to all delegates (except speakers and those mentioned below) and include follow-up information. For example:

- Thank people for attending.
- Link to online notes and actions required.
- Link to the online survey and include a deadline.
- Link to other information/documentation.
- Announce forthcoming events or other news.
- Remind them to send in their invoice or expenses claim and include a deadline of about two weeks (if paying delegate expenses).

To anyone who helped or was involved in an emergency

Send a personal note of appreciation to anyone who assisted you, such as colleagues or delegates who stepped into the breach. Also, should anyone have been involved in an accident or taken ill during the event, send an email or note enquiring after their health. For example:

- Thank people for their assistance or enquire after their health.
- Link to online notes and actions required (if appropriate).
- Link to the online survey and include a deadline (if appropriate).
- Link to other information/documentation (if appropriate).
- Announce forthcoming events or other news (if appropriate).
- Remind them to send in their invoice or expenses claim and include a deadline of about two weeks (if paying delegate expenses).

After that flurry of email writing, there will only be one more to write: a reminder to complete the feedback form a couple of days before closing the survey (see **Survey** p.126).

Build a mailing list

A pool of potential speakers and delegates is worth its weight in gold. Therefore, add everyone who attended or expressed an interest in the event to a dedicated mailing list. For example, details can be stored and managed in a spreadsheet, dedicated address book in your email client, CRM (Customer Relationship Management) system, or email marketing service, such as **MailChimp**[8]. This will make the next hunt for speakers and delegates much easier.

---

[8] http://mailchimp.com/

Learn from the event

There's always room for improvement, so use the feedback from the online survey to structure future events, but be cautious about focussing on the negative comments only. There will always be someone who didn't like the food, venue, speakers, you name it, even when everyone else raved about it.

It's impossible to please everyone. I once ran a national event in the central Midlands at a venue that was less than ten minutes' walk from one of the biggest rail interchanges in the country. One delegate complained that the location was too far away from his home town (just over an hour's train ride away).

However, some negative comments should be taken seriously, particularly if the venue wasn't to most people's liking or a particular speaker wasn't deemed to be relevant. I once booked a speaker who wasn't part of the academic community, but who was passionate about the work he was doing. His enthusiasm came across in his rapid speech. Feedback from some of the delegates focused on his lack of presentation skills rather than on the content itself. When invited back to speak at another event, I asked if he would slow down a little. There was no negative feedback on that occasion.

However, be aware that business or academic rivalries can result in negative comments, no matter how brilliant the session.

As well as examining the feedback, conduct your own analysis of the event. Take some time to reflect on where improvements could have been made and make a note for next time. Think about the suitability of the agenda, speakers, location, venue, catering, and whether the aims and benefits were achieved. Consider any issues that arose and what you learnt from them. How can you do better next time?

And now to the final checklist!

Follow-up checklist

Just a few more days to go before the event can be completely tied off. This checklist is also a timetable itemising what you need to do after the event. Depending on your event's requirements, not every item will be of relevance.

Day 1 (Day after the event)

Survey
- Set up the online survey (this could also be done during the organising stage).
- Conduct your own analysis of the event.

Notes
- Write up or edit notes and actions. If you have permission to do so, post online or send as an email attachment.

Thank you notes
- Thank your contact and staff at the venue for their assistance.
- Thank speakers for their presentation/session.
- Thank delegates for attending.
- Thank everyone who helped or was involved in an emergency.

Build a mailing list
- Add everyone who attended or expressed an interest in the event to a dedicated mailing list.

Day 5

Survey
- Email everyone to remind them to complete the survey.

Day 7

Survey
- Close the survey.
- Analyse the survey results.
- Learn where you can make improvements for next time.

That was the last checklist, but just before you go…

AND FINALLY...

Chapter 23

AND FINALLY...

By planning, organising, and running an event, you've had the honour of bringing people together. You've been instrumental in providing the environment for people to collaborate, share, bond, and network. And whilst not everyone appreciates or is aware of the sheer amount of hard work that goes into making an event run smoothly, I do hope the *Prepare to Meet* process has made planning and organising your meeting easier and less stressful.

May all your events be successful!

About The Author

Sharon Perry spent twelve years in the university sector working in project management and supporting communities of practice. She was also responsible for planning, organising and facilitating meetings, workshops, mini-conferences, and project management events.

Sharon has never forgotten her first attempt at organising an event and wrote this book, because she would have loved a step-by-step guide like *Prepare to Meet* at the time.

Visit **http://www.stressfreemeeting.com** for more information or follow **@preparetomeet** on Twitter.

www.ingramcontent.com/pod-product-compliance
Lightning Source LLC
Chambersburg PA
CBHW071443180526
45170CB00001B/435